Edibles: Fun Food to Color

By Robin Joy Andreae

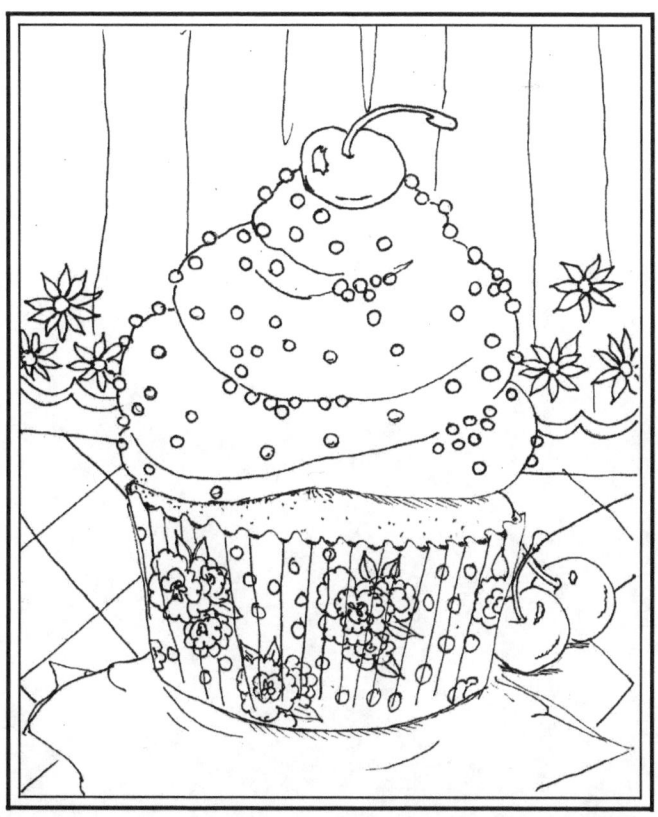

ISBN-10: **1523992557**
ISBN-13: **978-1523992553**

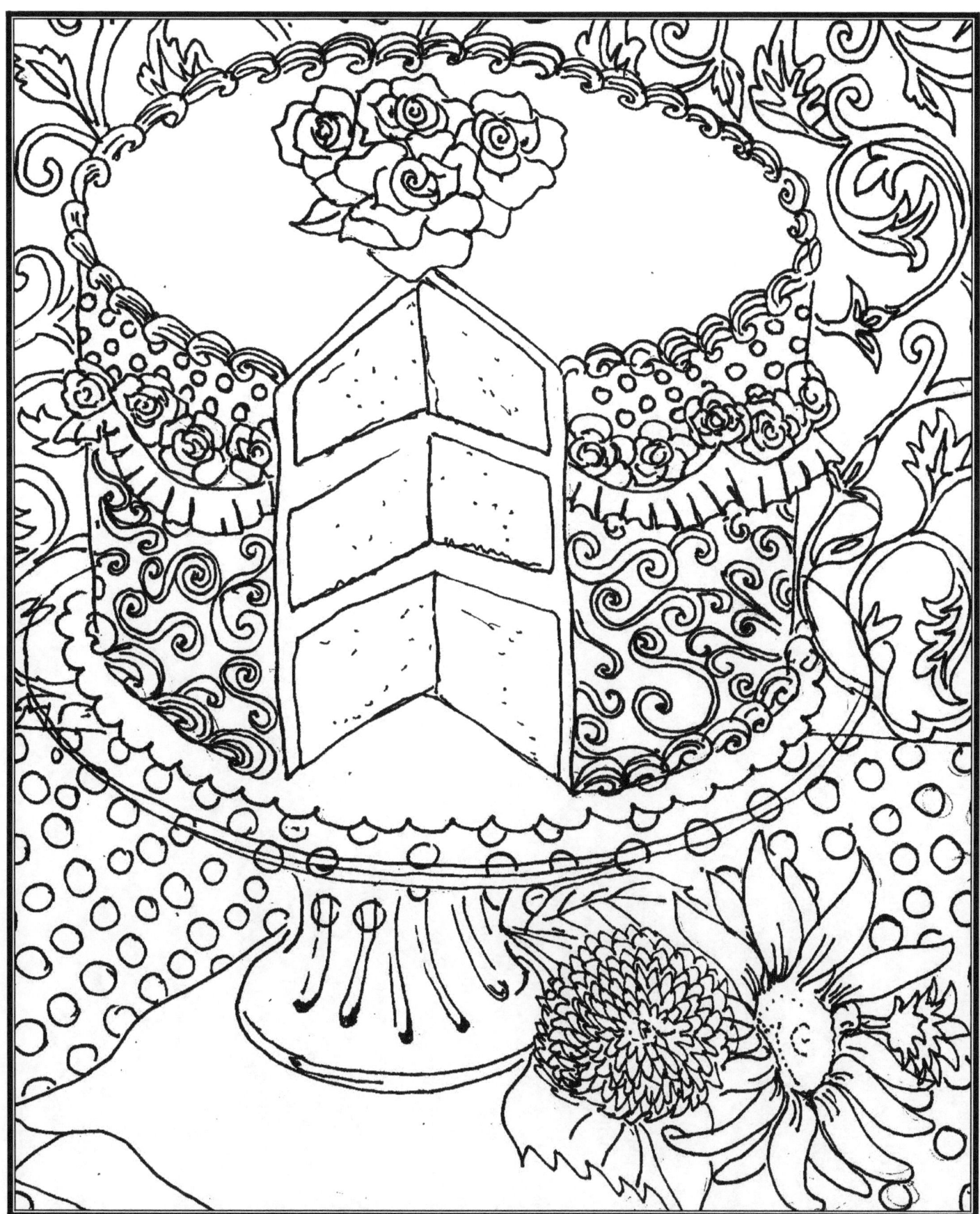

Figure 1 Decadent Triple Layer Cake

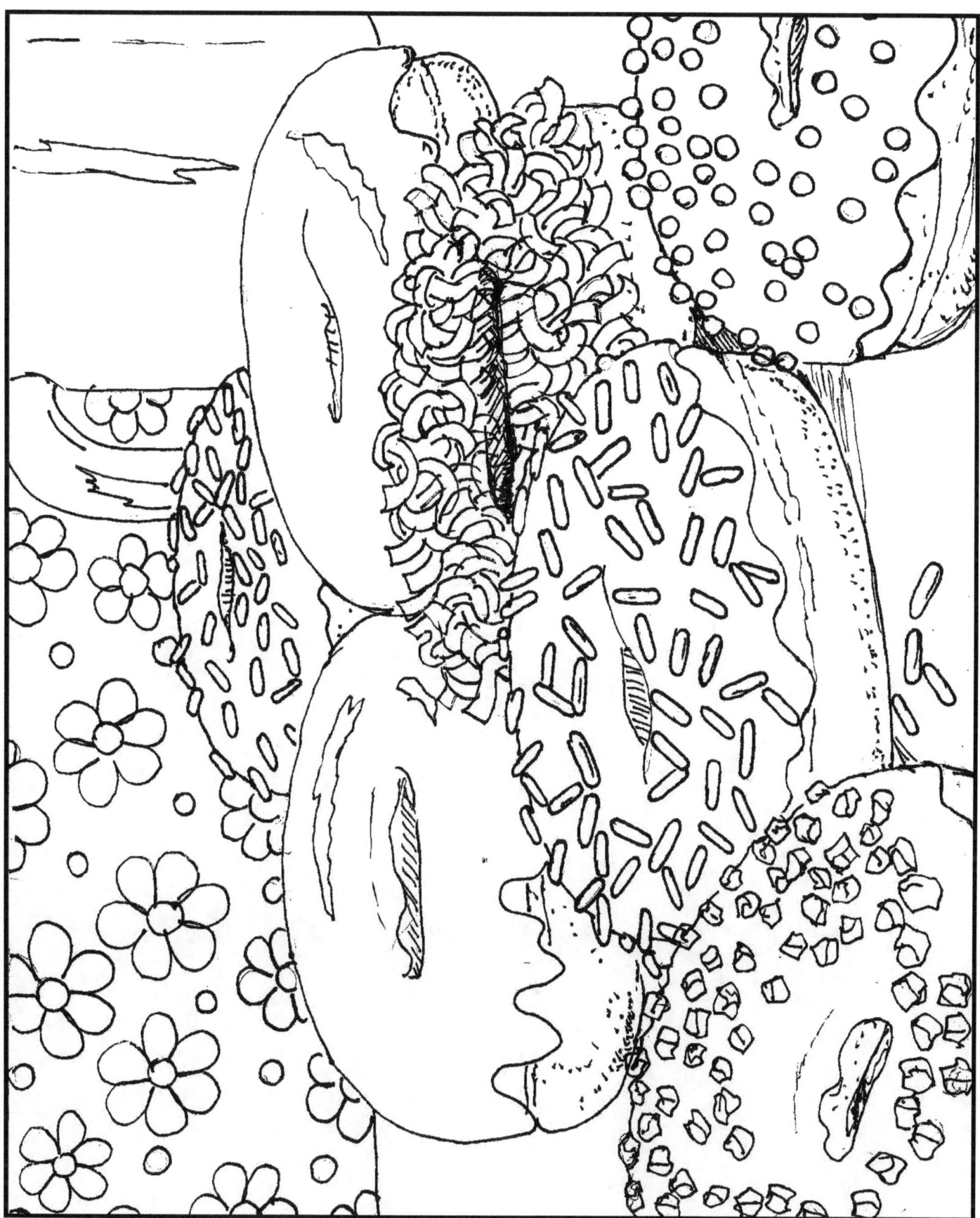

Figure 2 Doughnuts

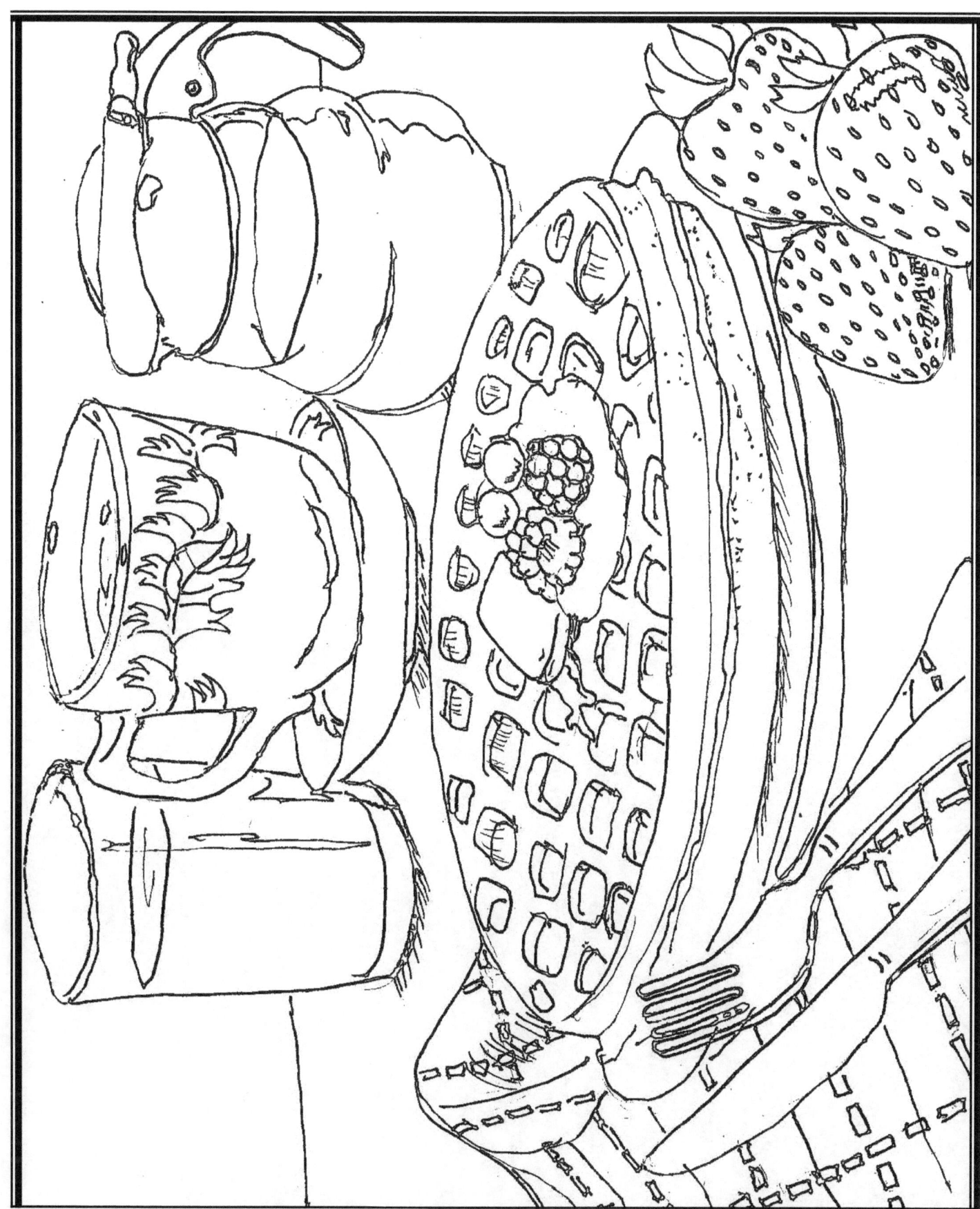

Figure 3 Waffle, Coffee & Juice

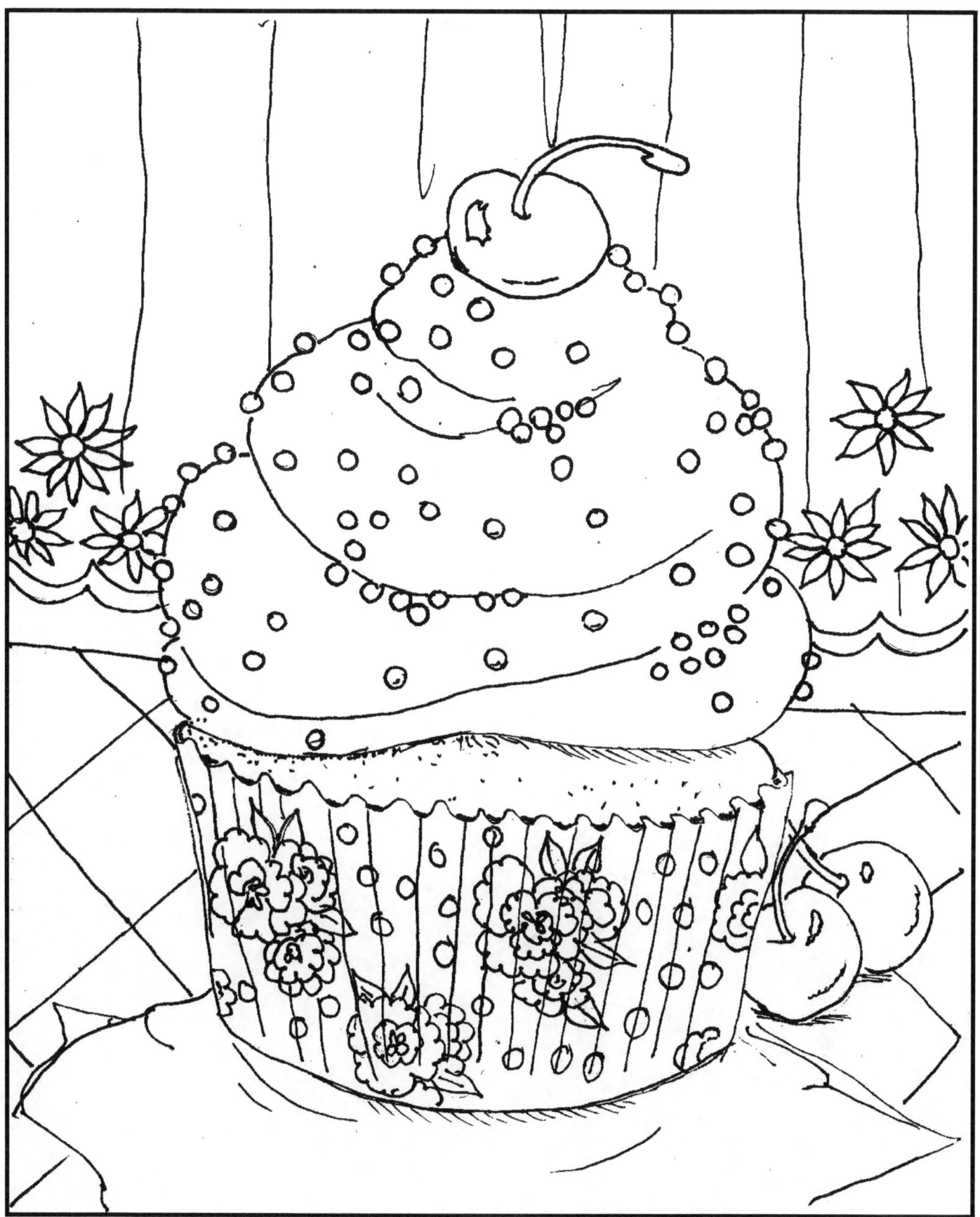

Figure 4 Cupcake

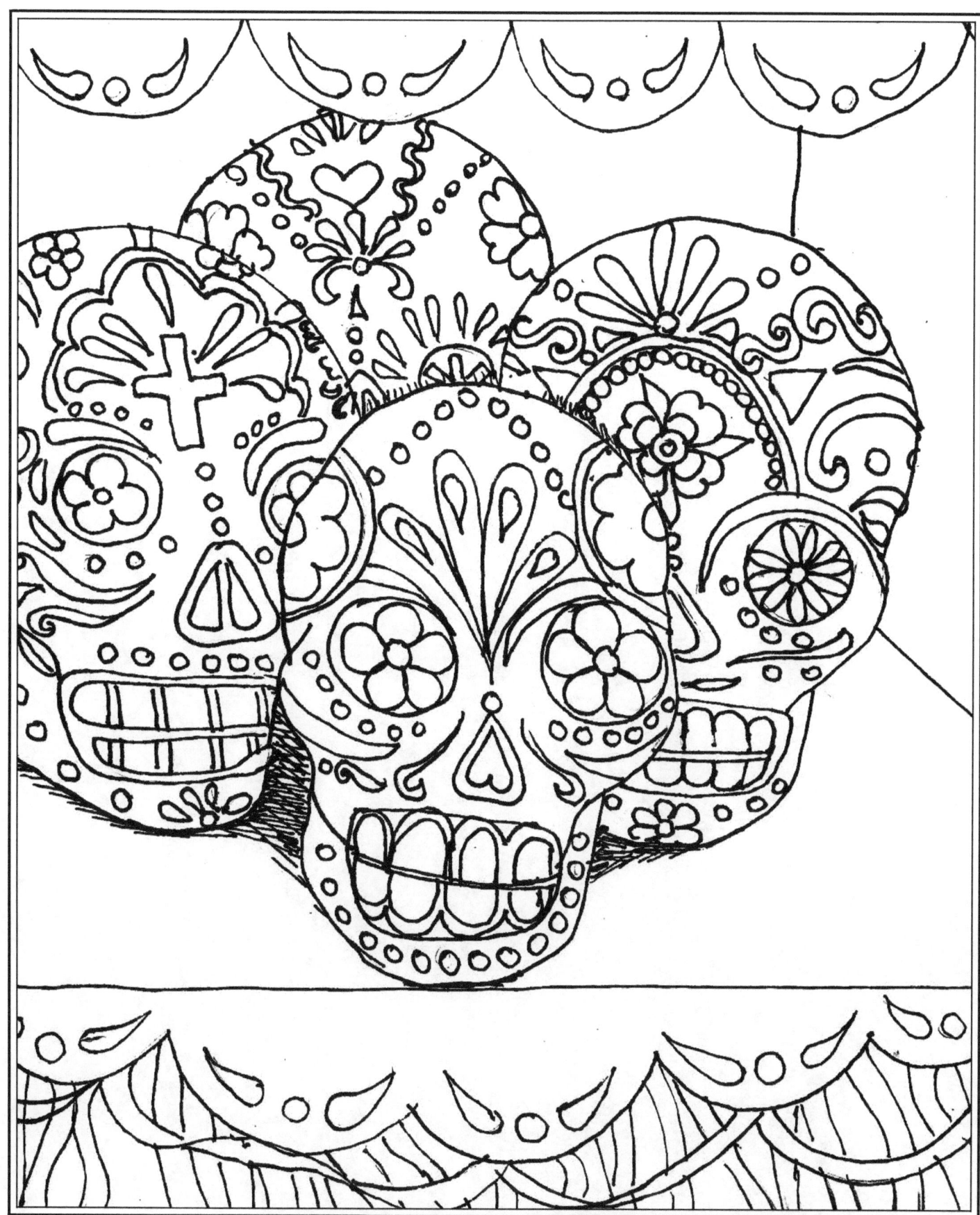

Figure 5 Day of the Dead Sugar Skulls

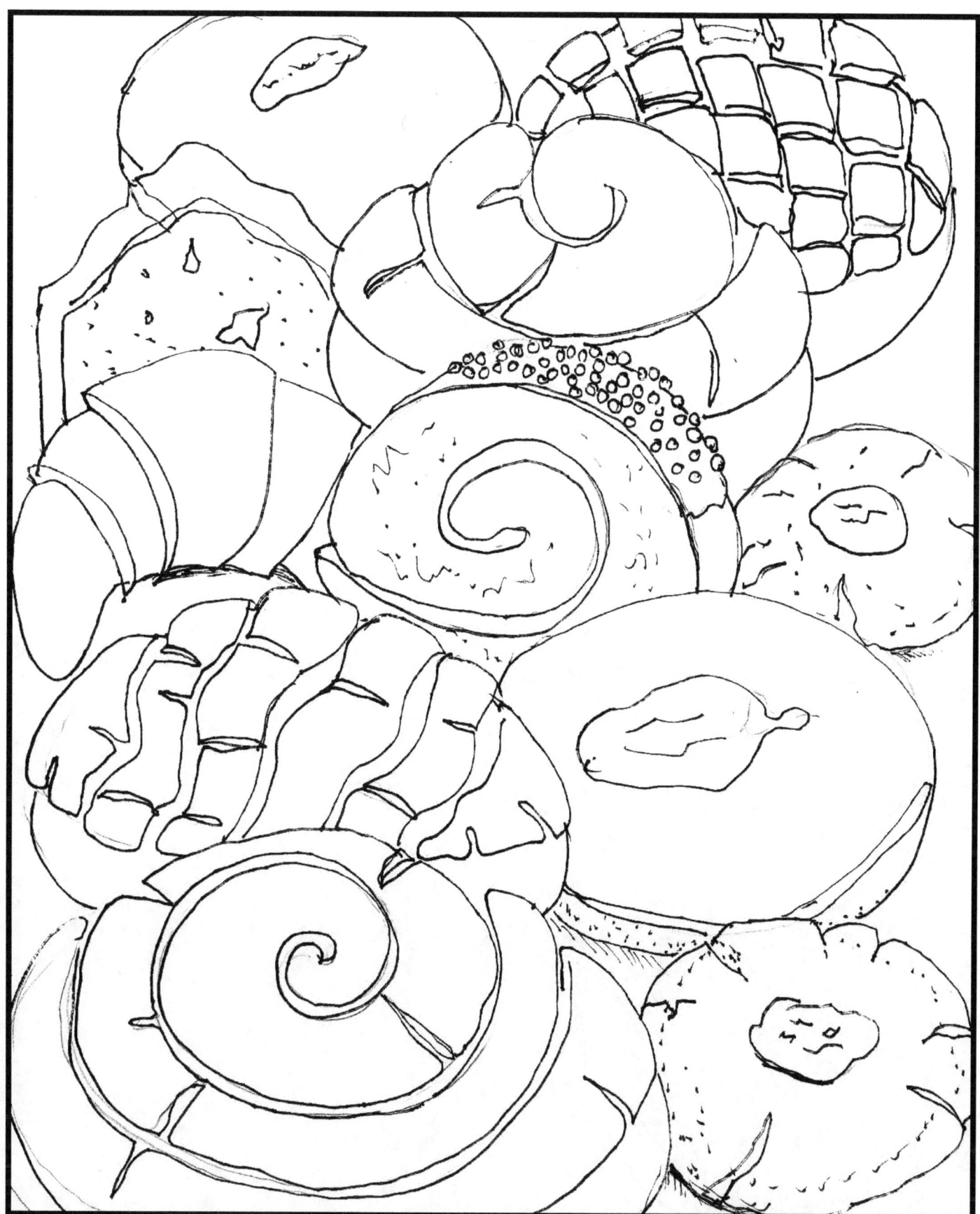

Figure 6 Mexican Pastries

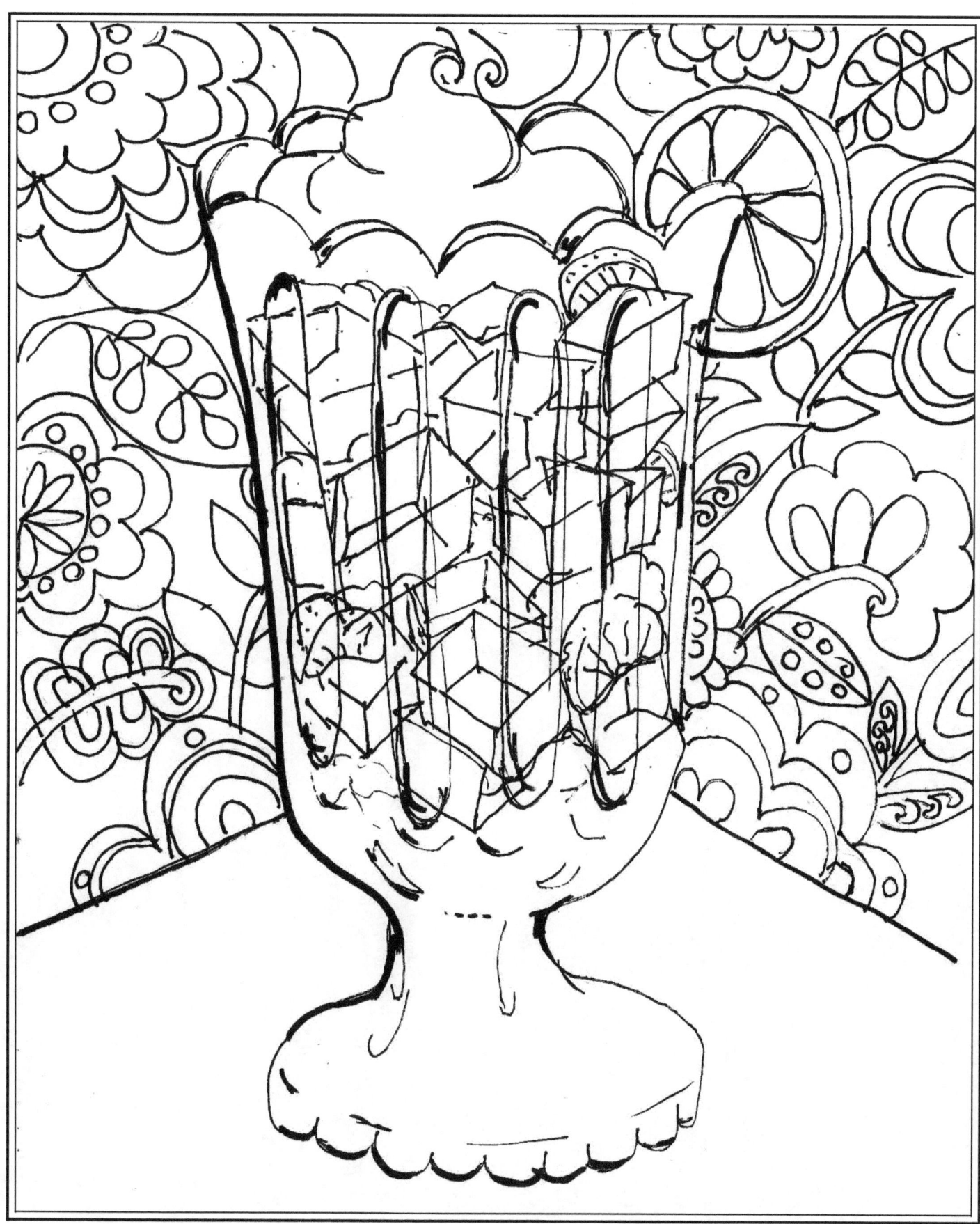

Figure 7 Jello Parfait

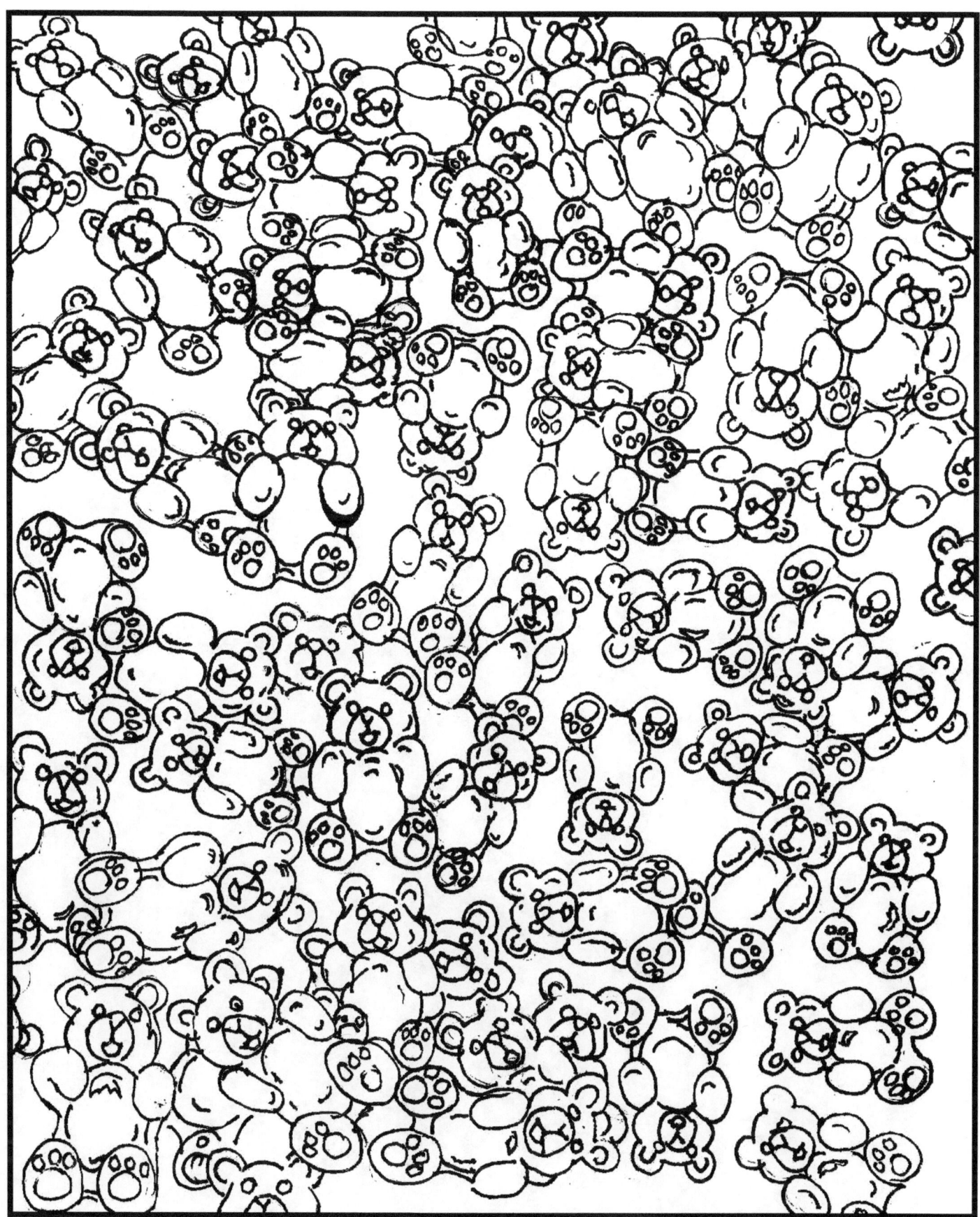

Figure 8 Gummy Bears

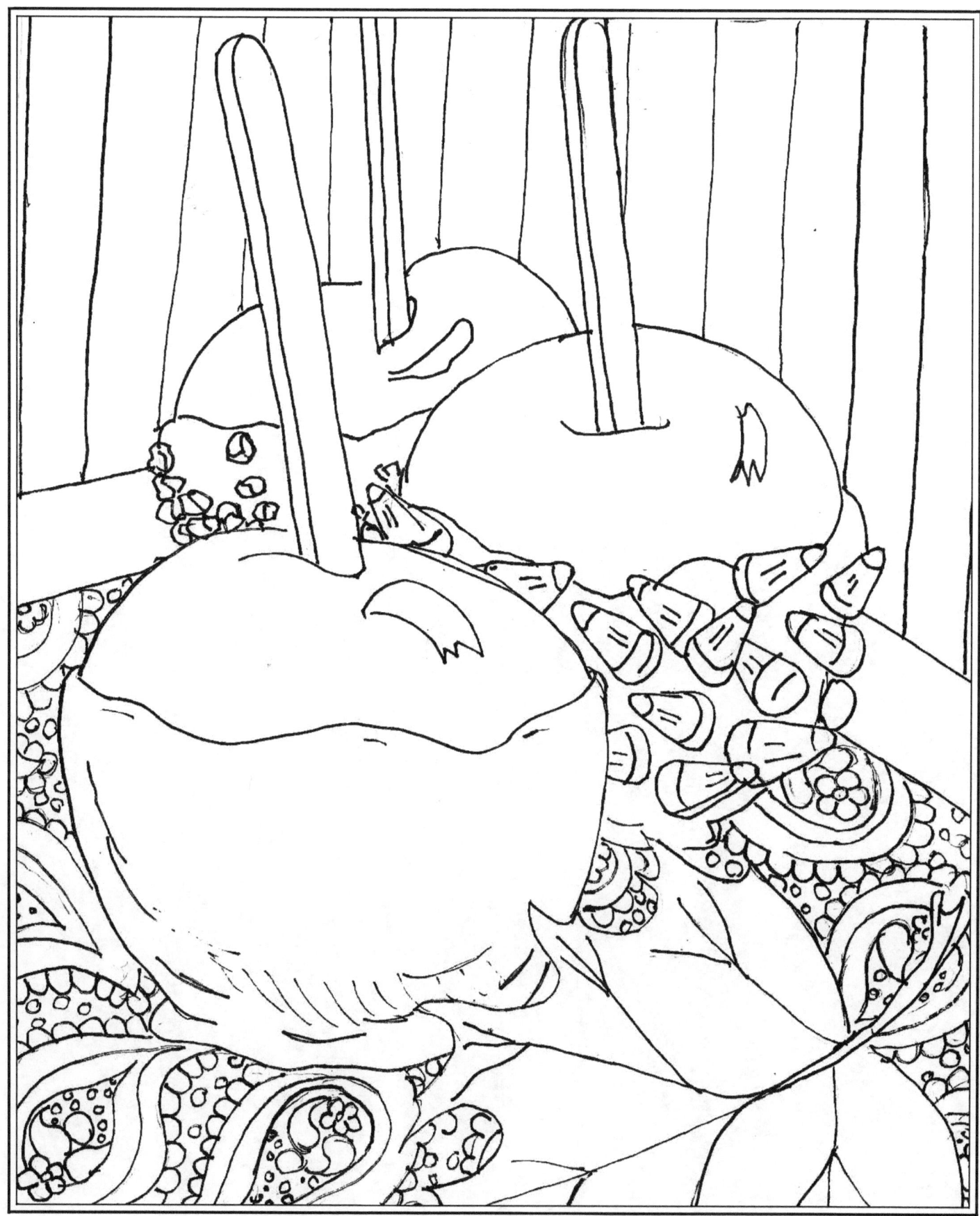

Figure 9 Candy Apples

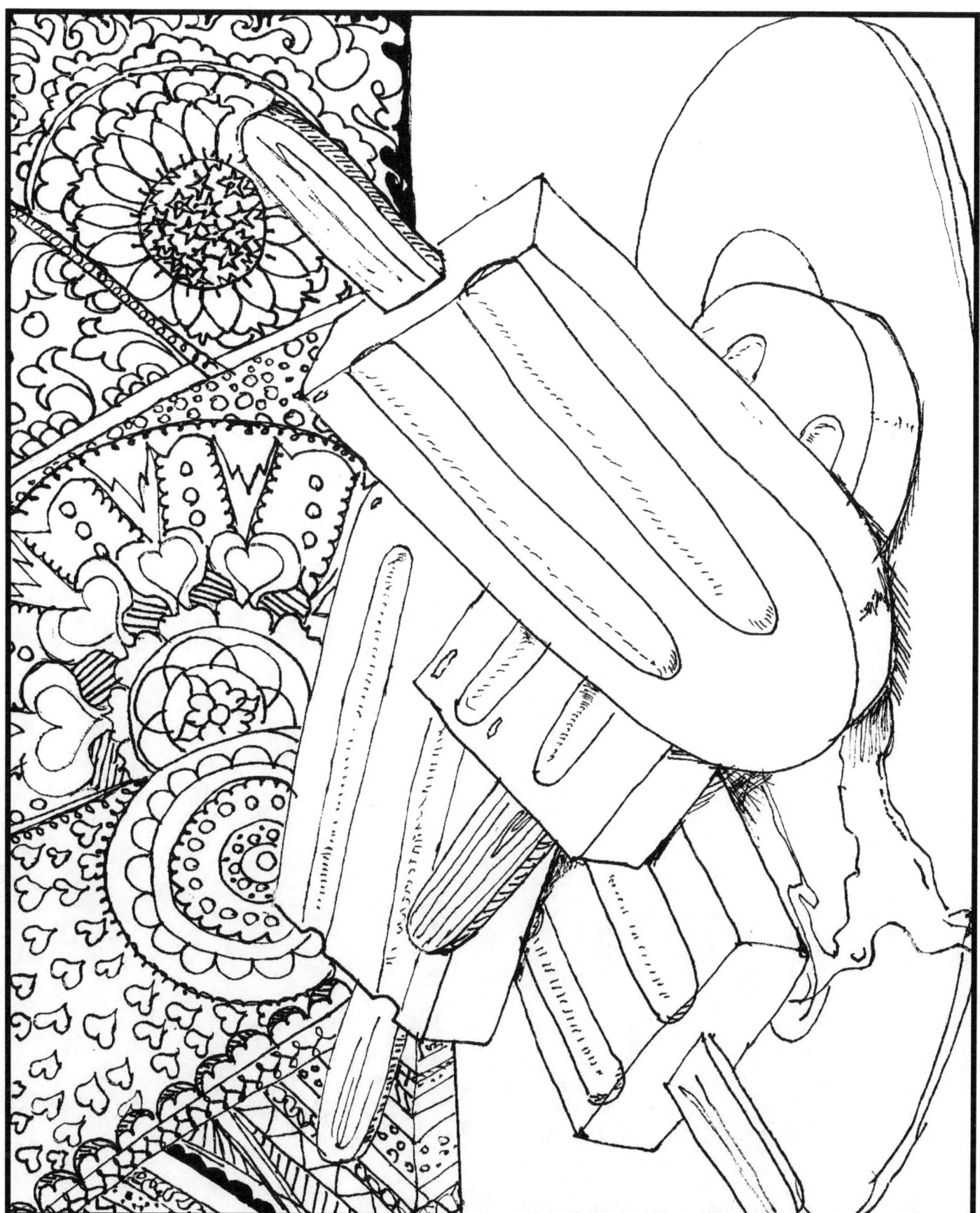

Figure 10 Popsicles

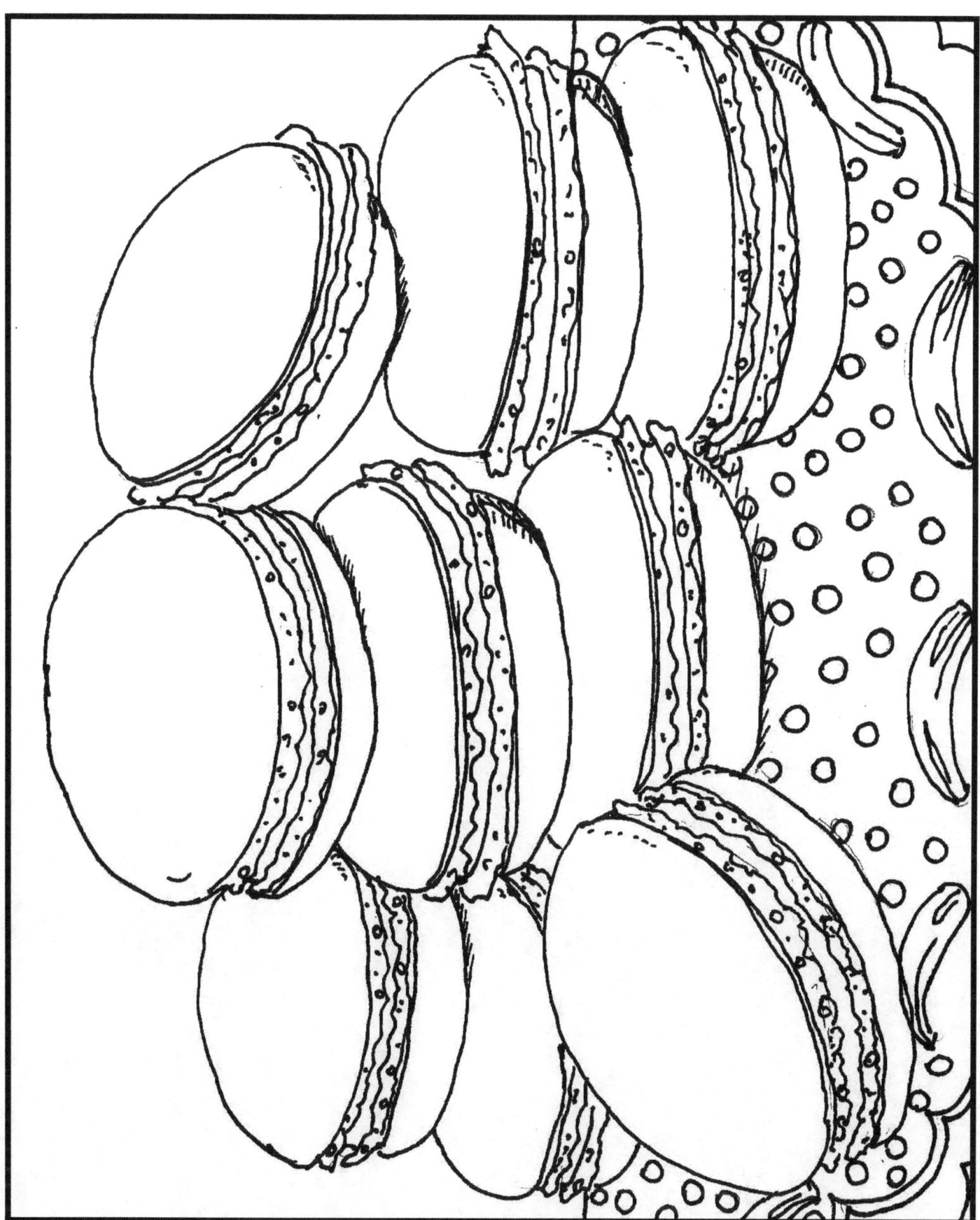

Figure 11 Macarons

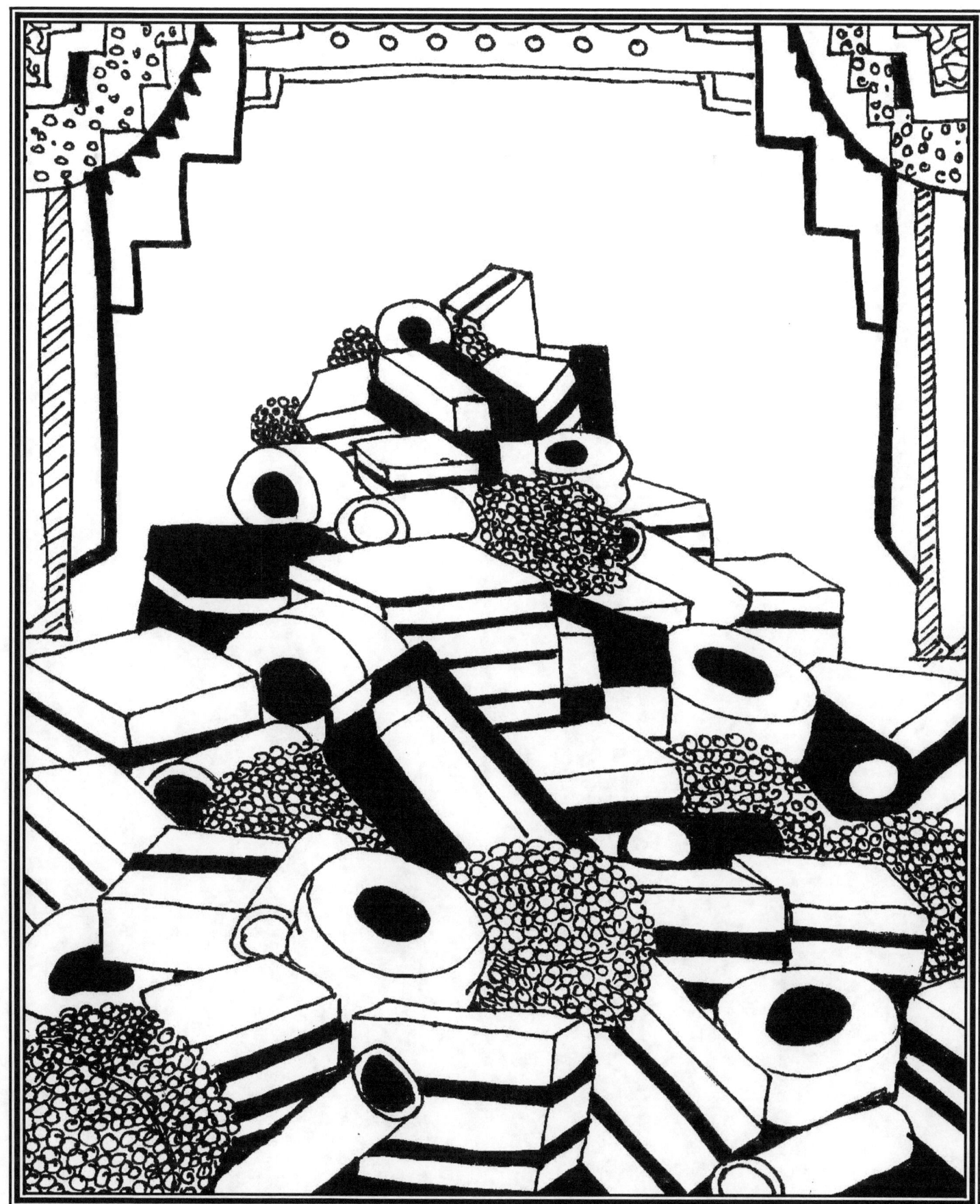

Figure 12 Licorice Allsorts

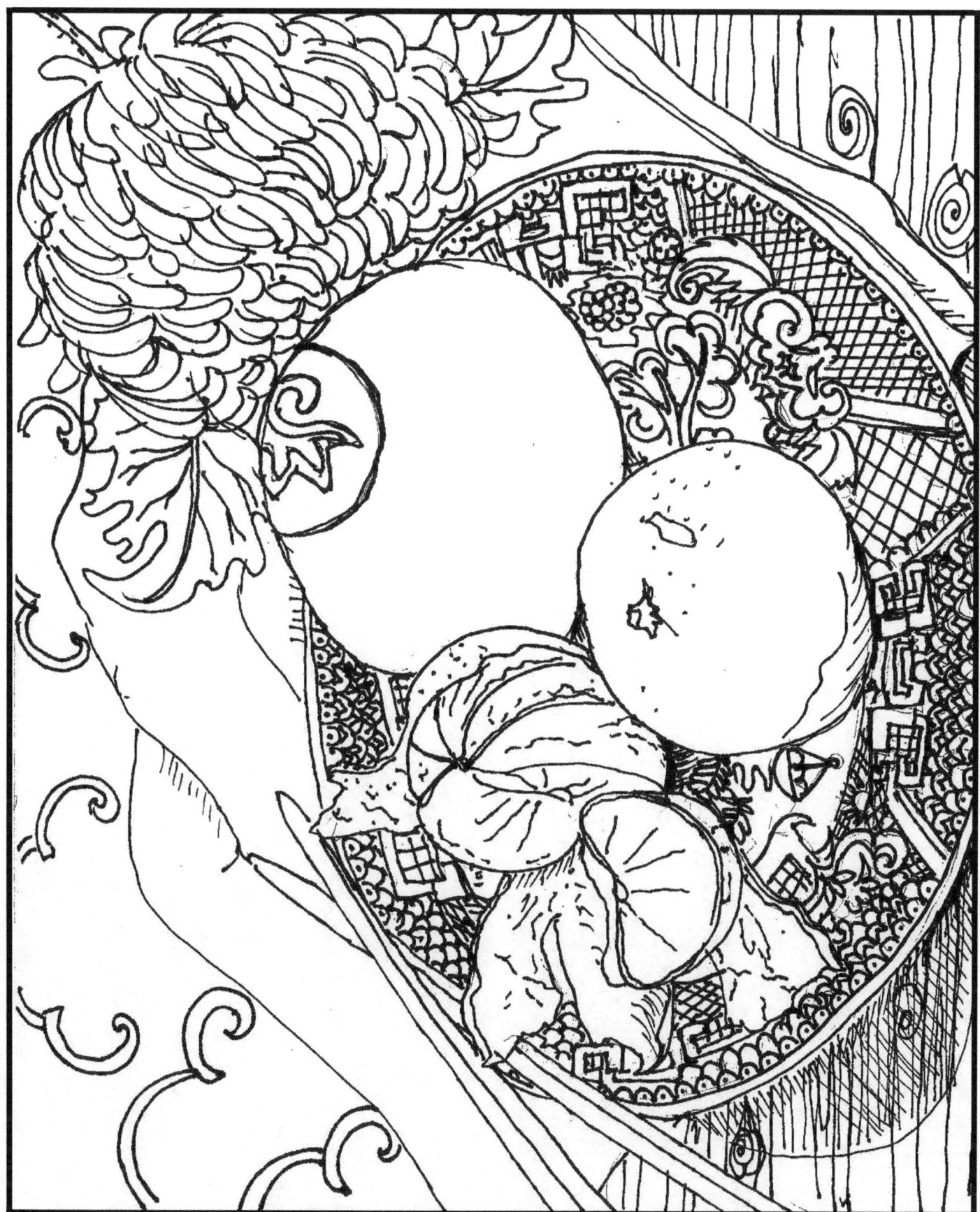

Figure 13 Mandarin Oranges and Black Bean Bun

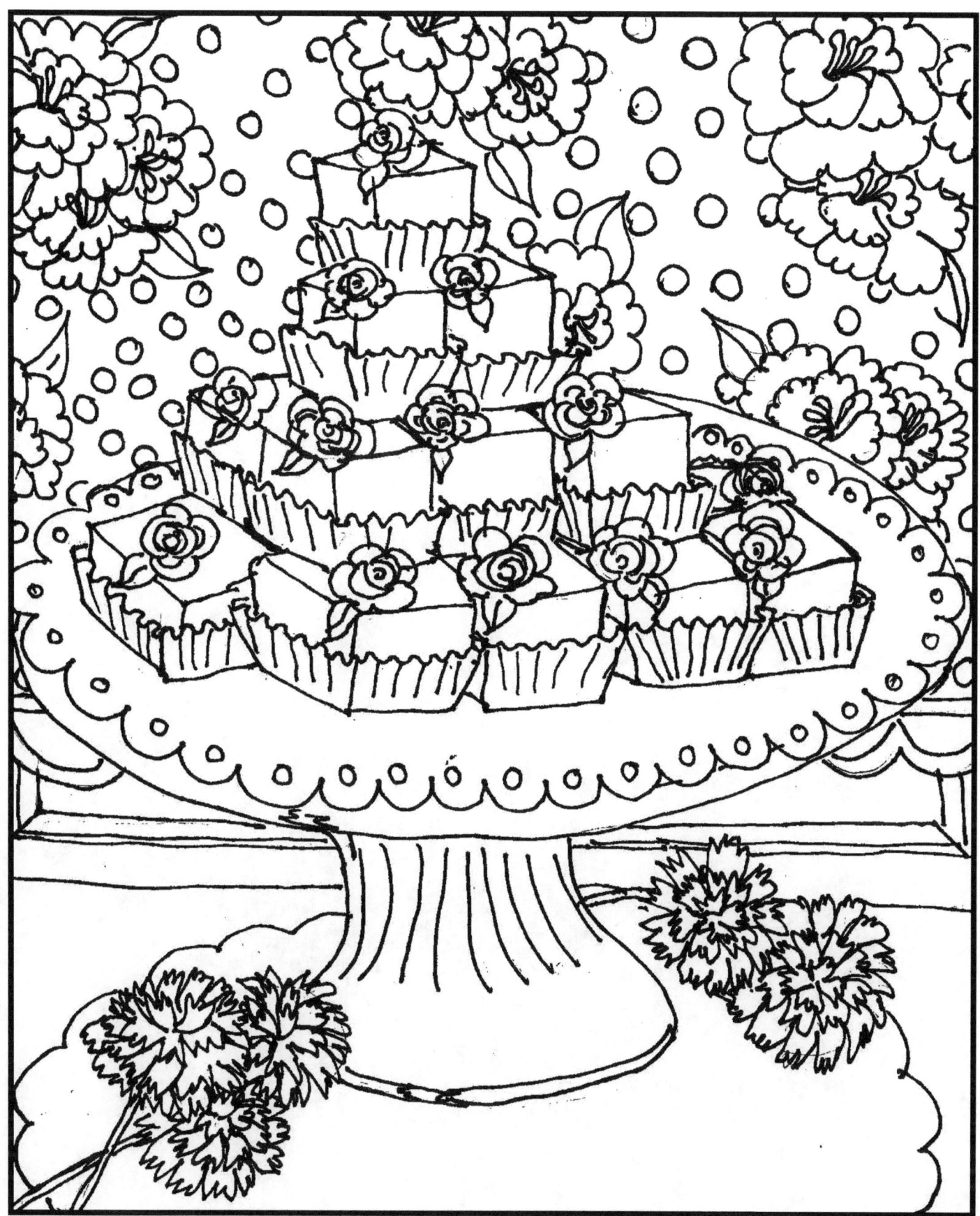

Figure 14 Petit Fours

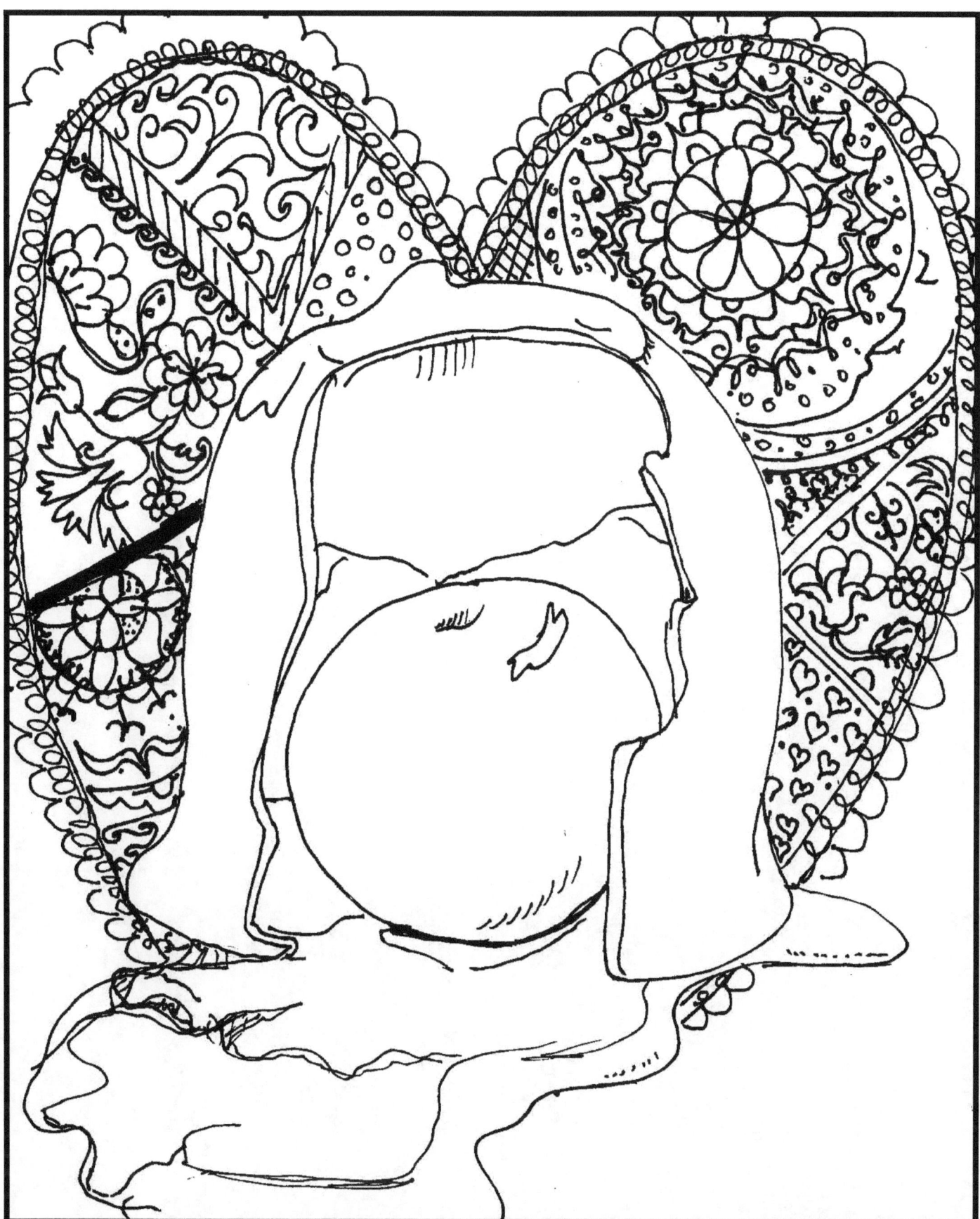

Figure 15 Chocolate Covered Cherry

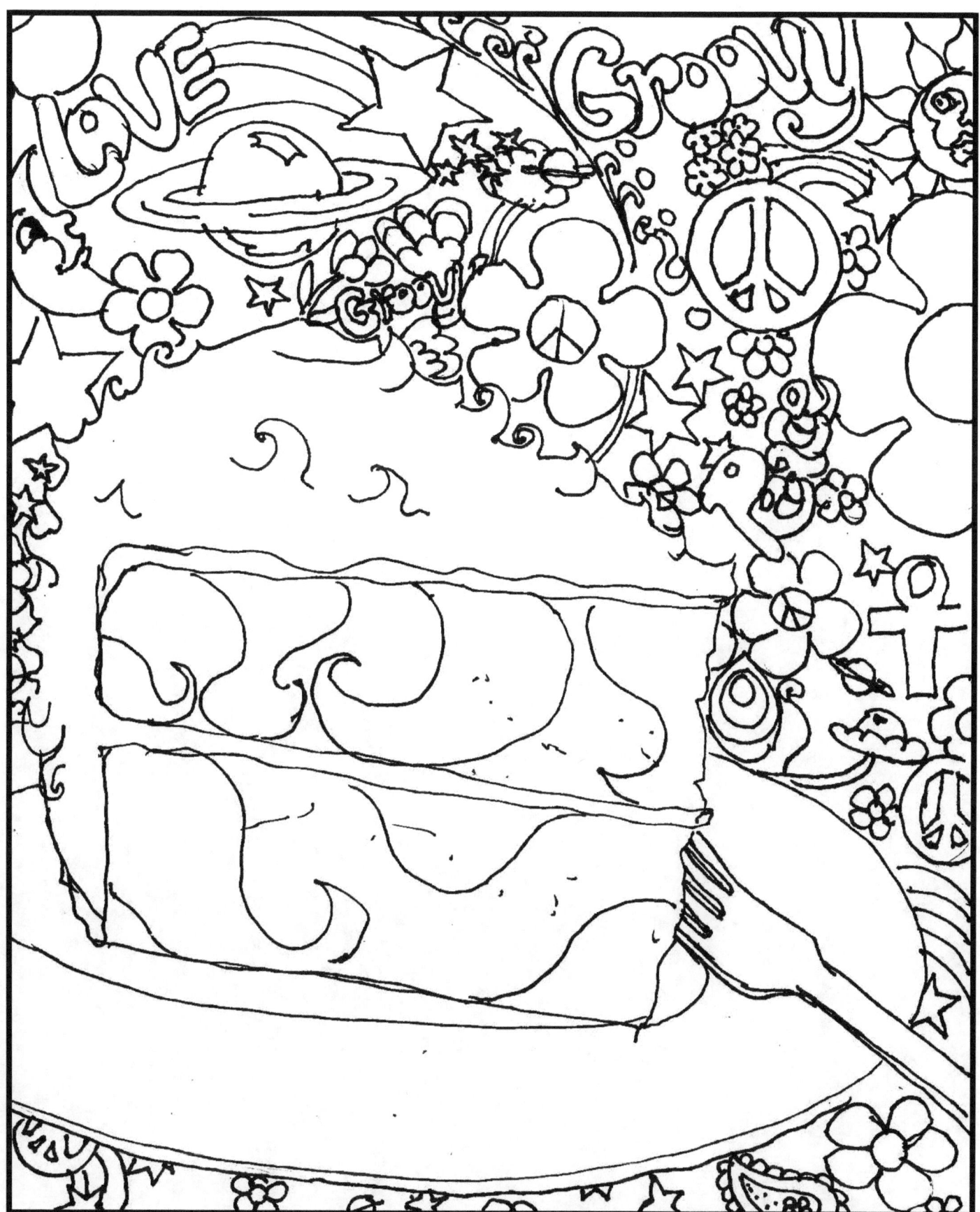

Figure 16 Groovy Tie Dye Cake

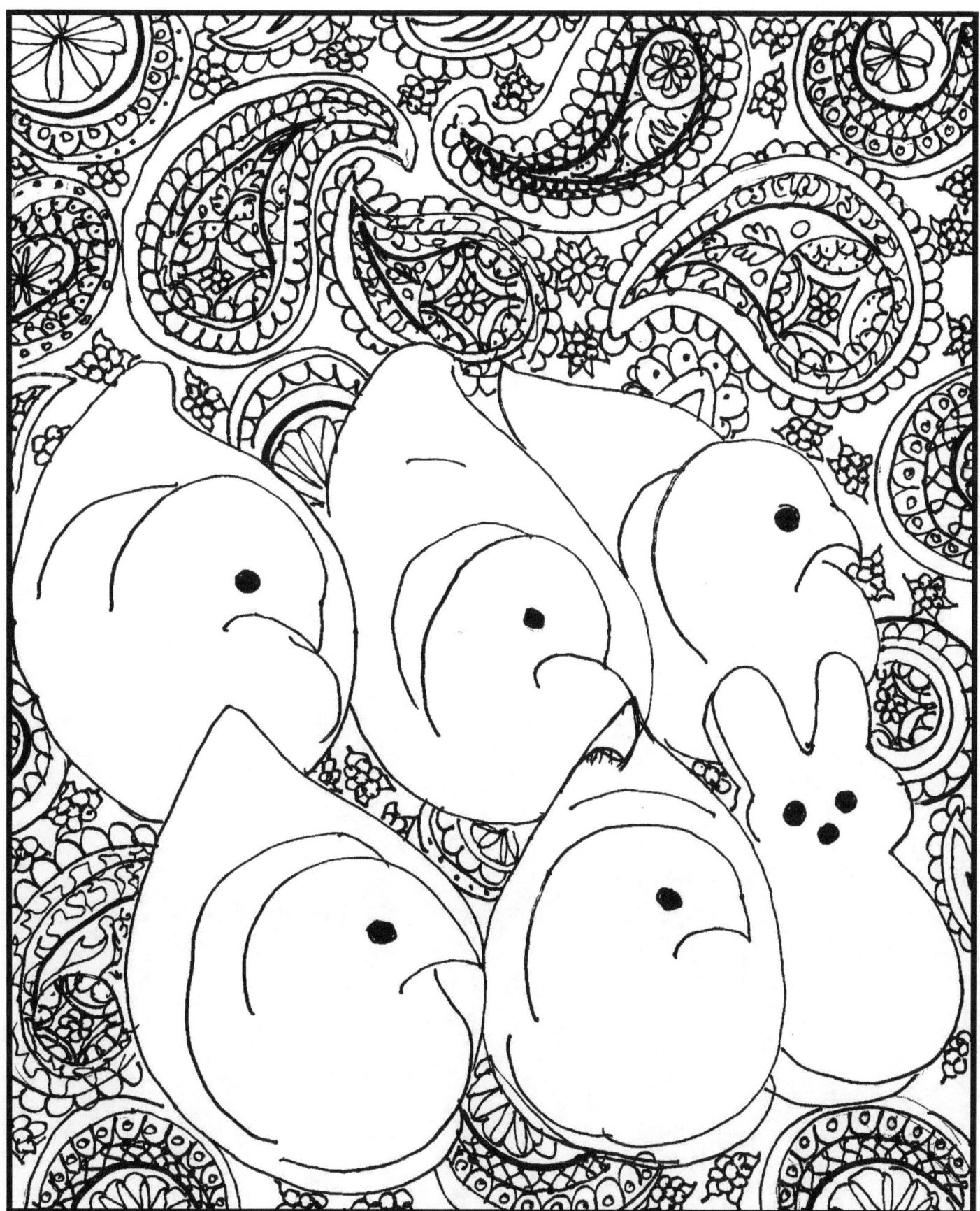

Figure 17 Peeps & Paisley

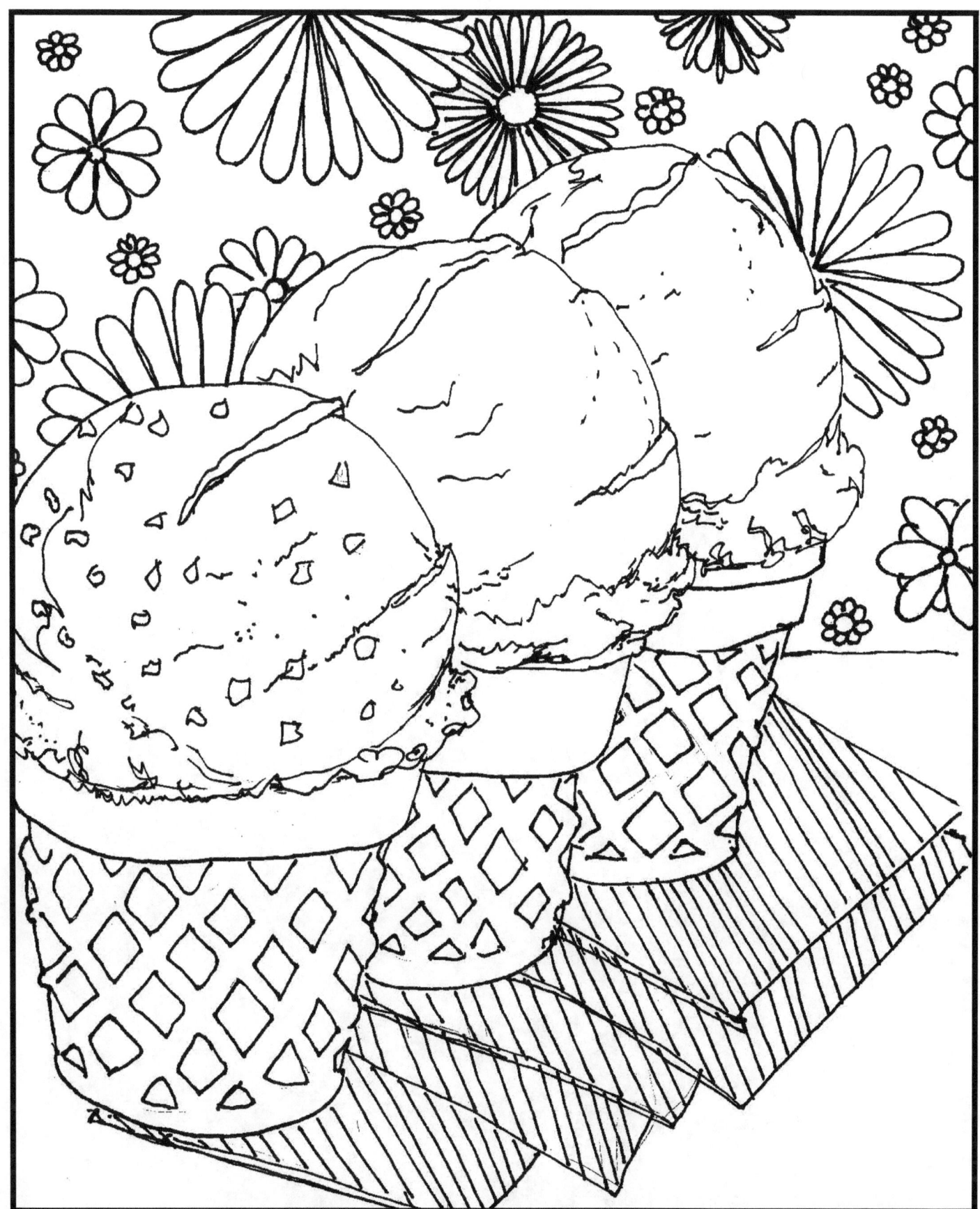

Figure 18 Ice Cream Cones

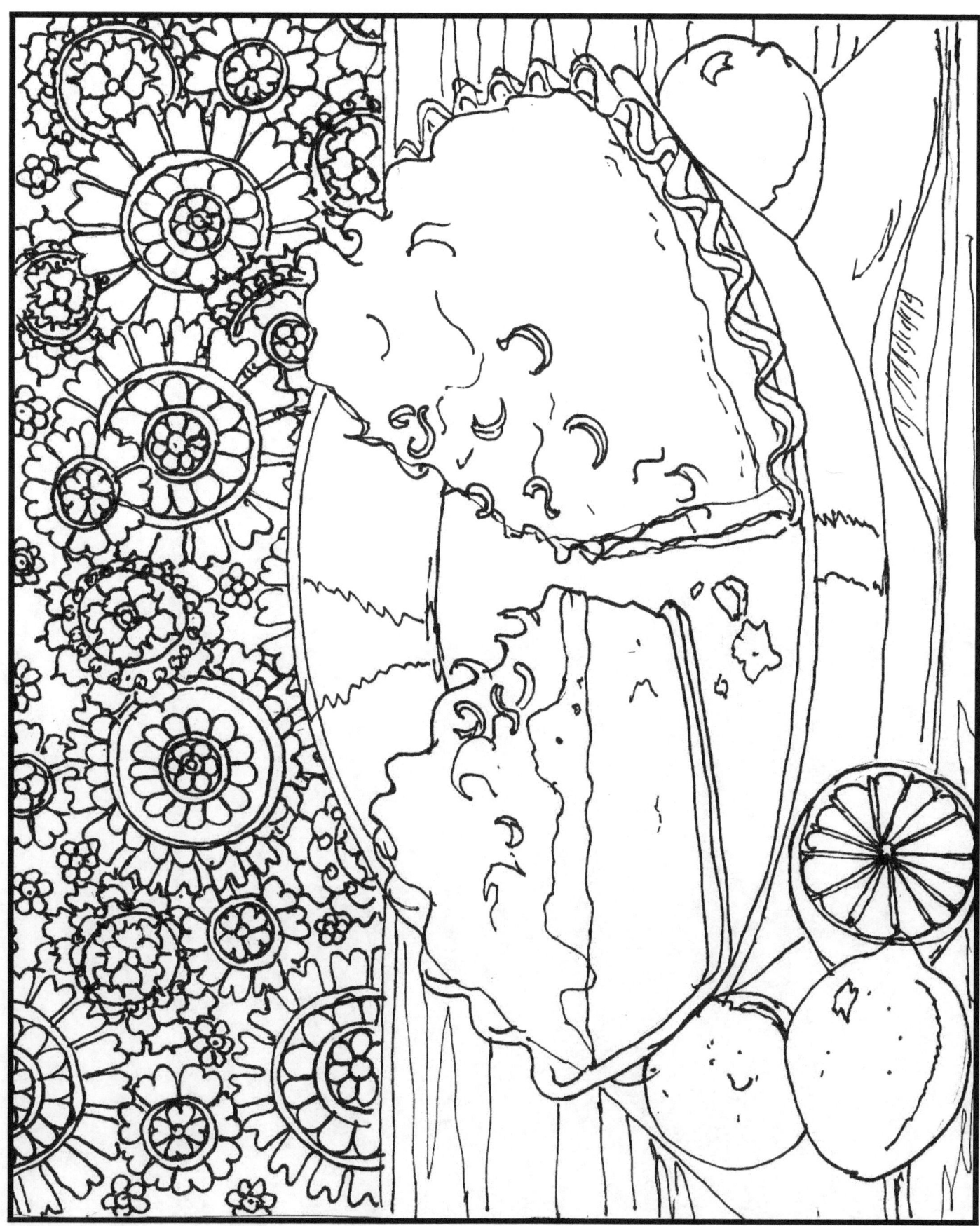

Figure 19 Lemon Meringue Pie

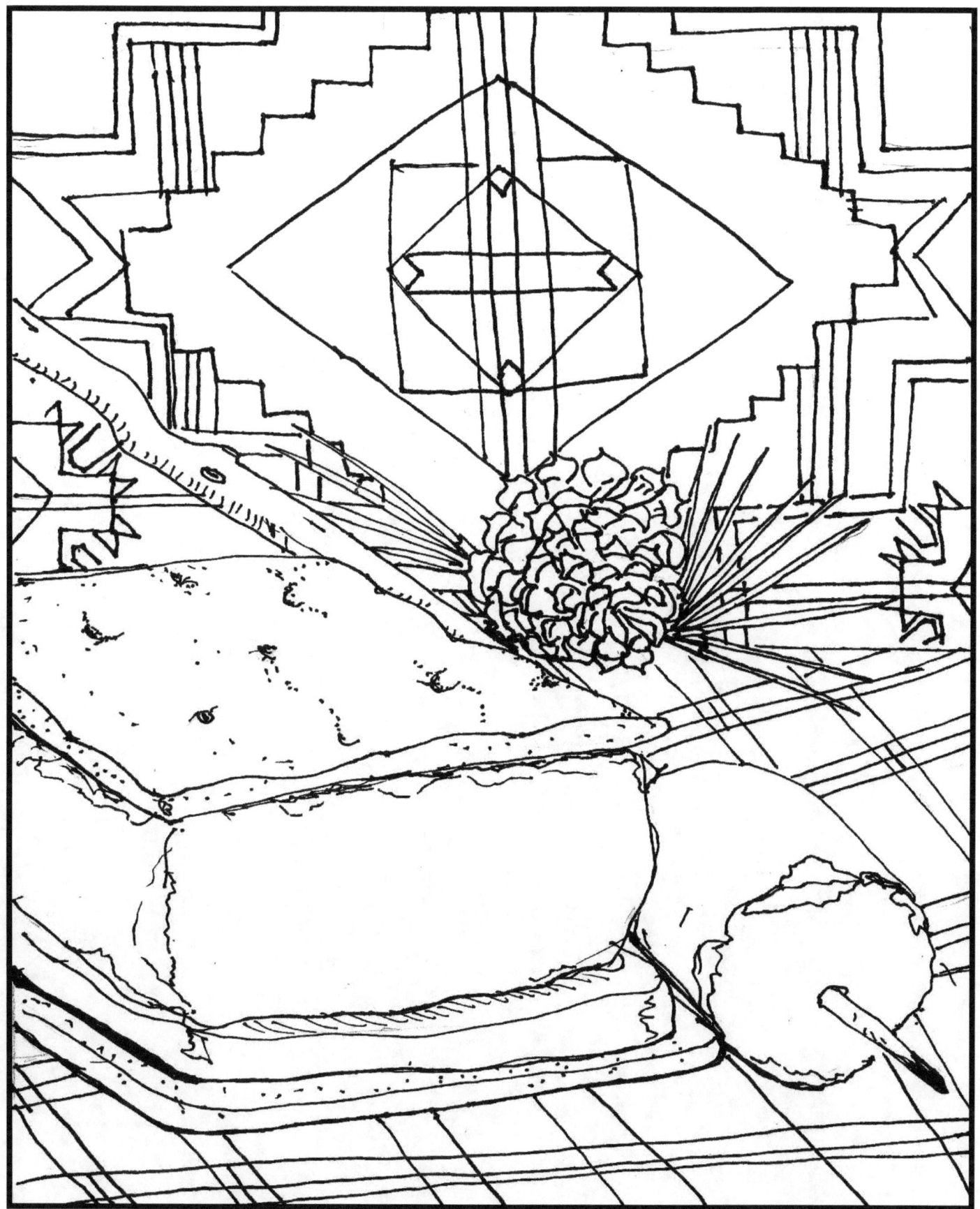

Figure 20 S'mores

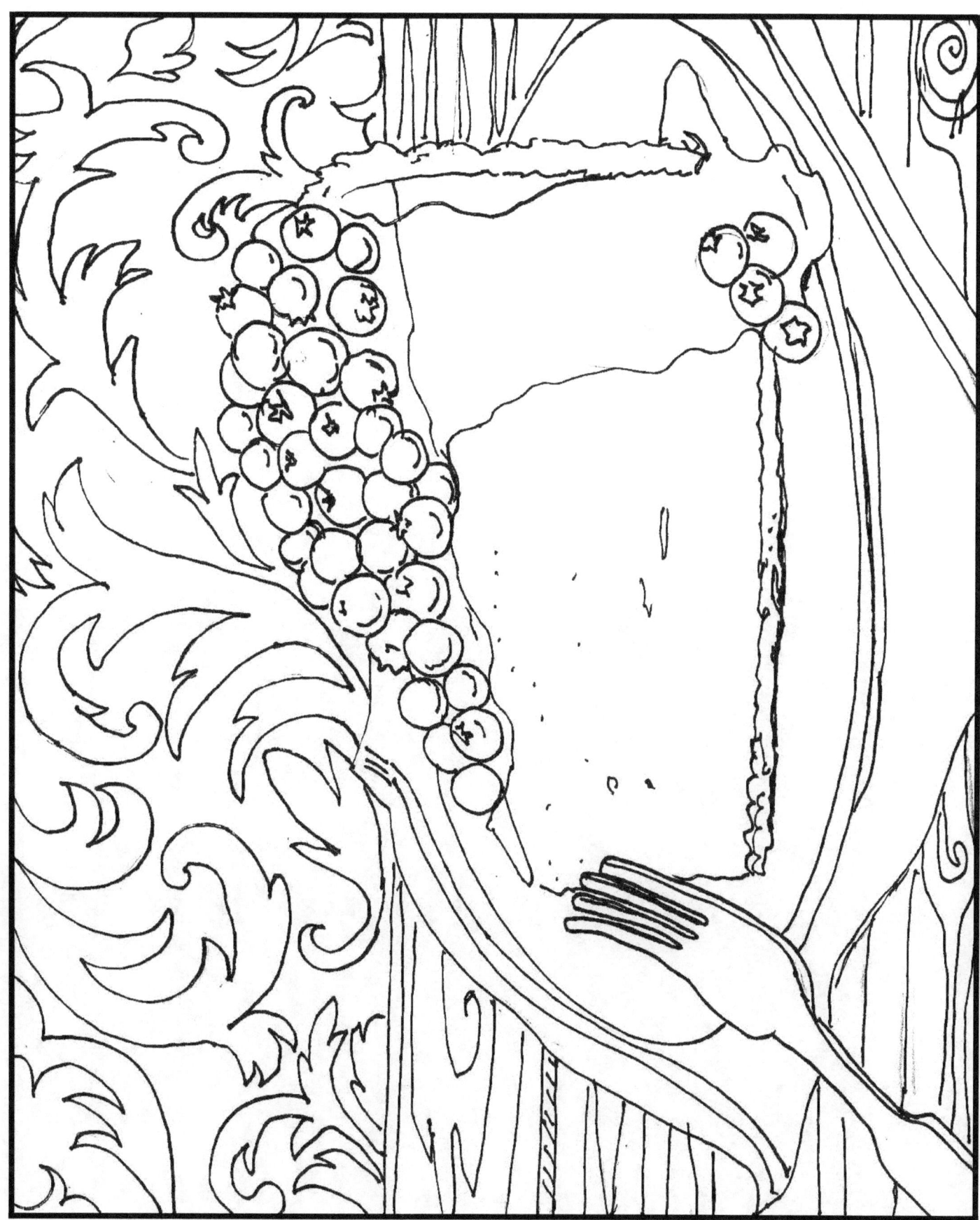

Figure 21 Blueberry Cheesecake

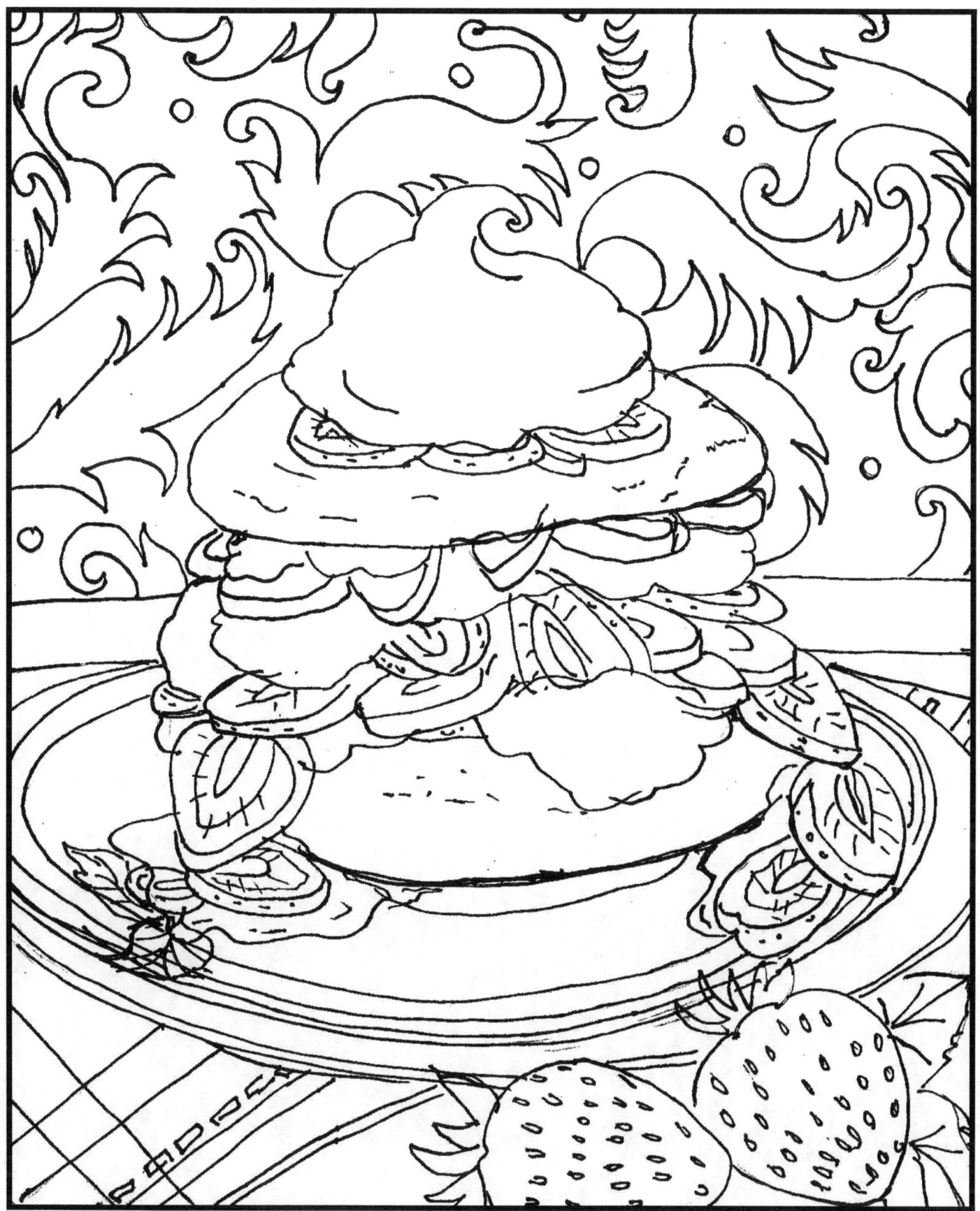

Figure 22 Strawberry Shortcake

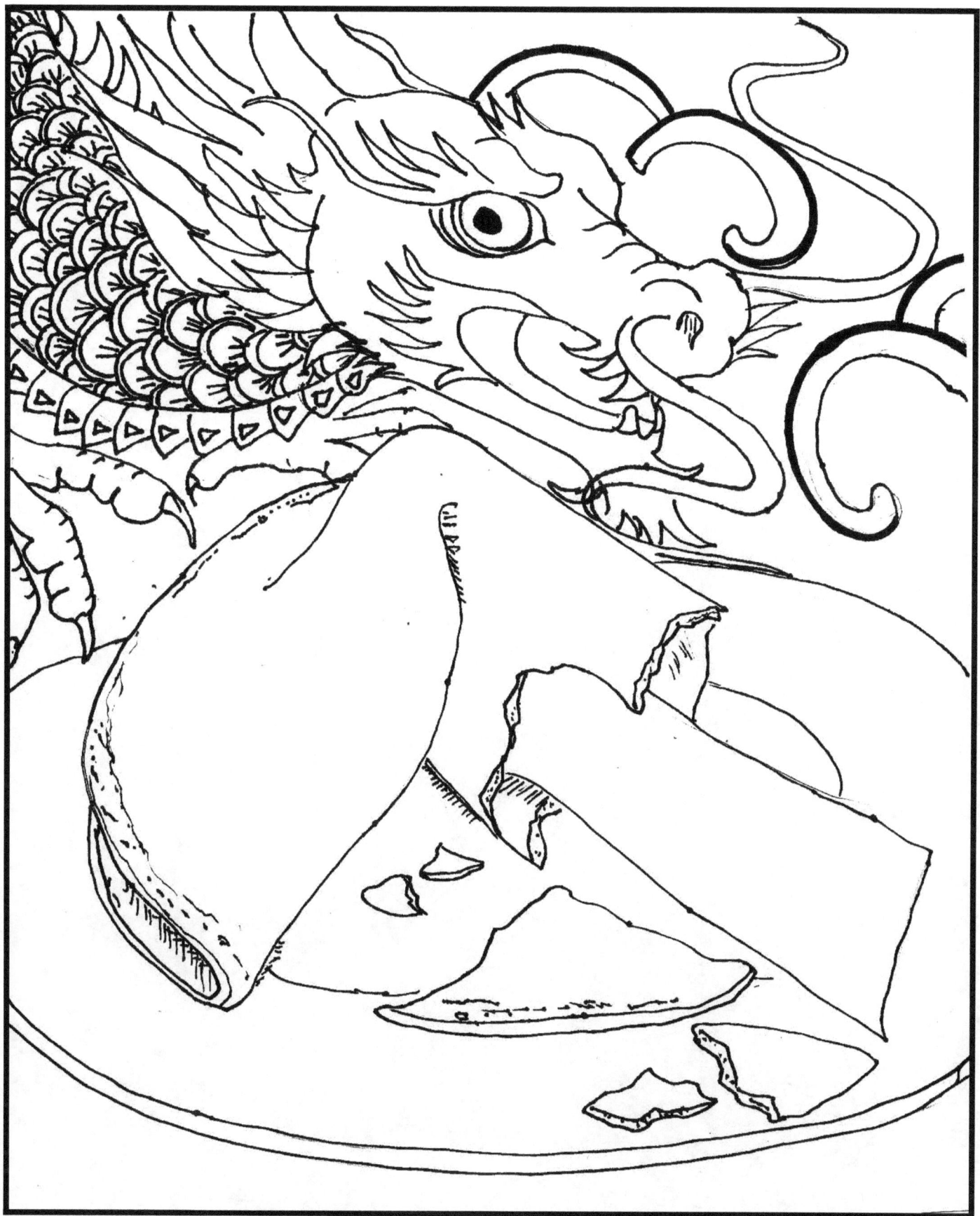

Figure 23 Write Your Fortune

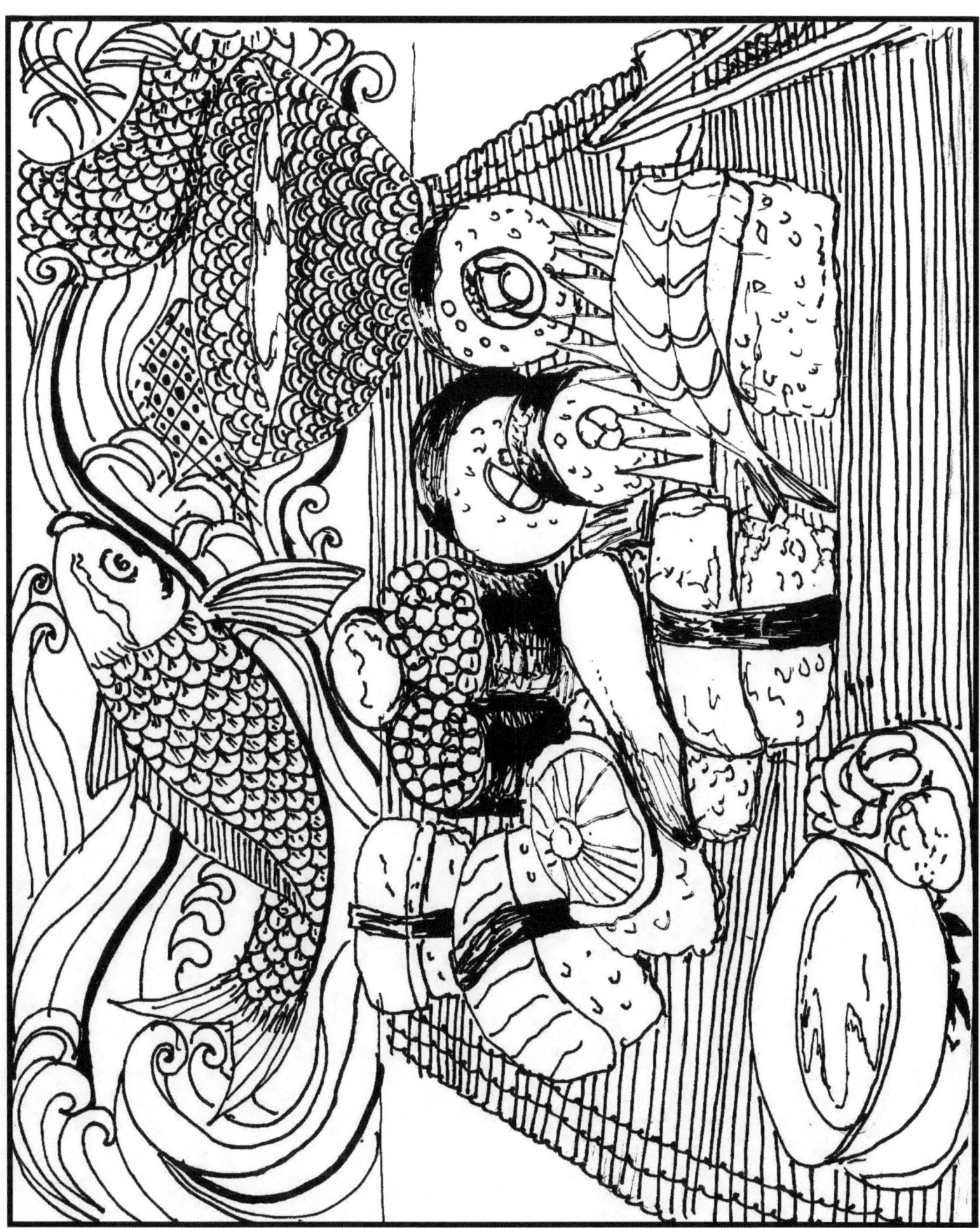

Figure 24 Sushi

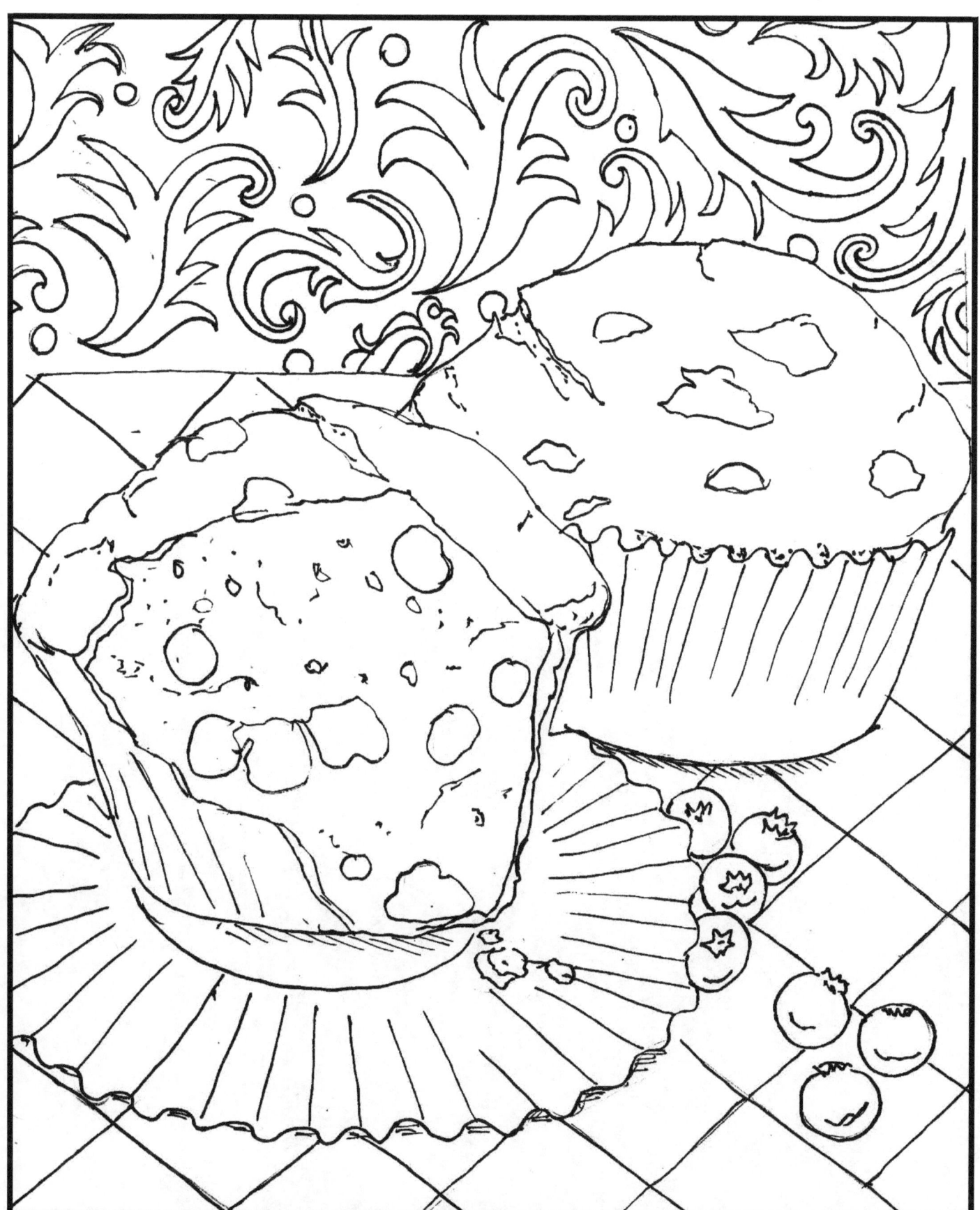

Figure 25 Blueberry Muffins

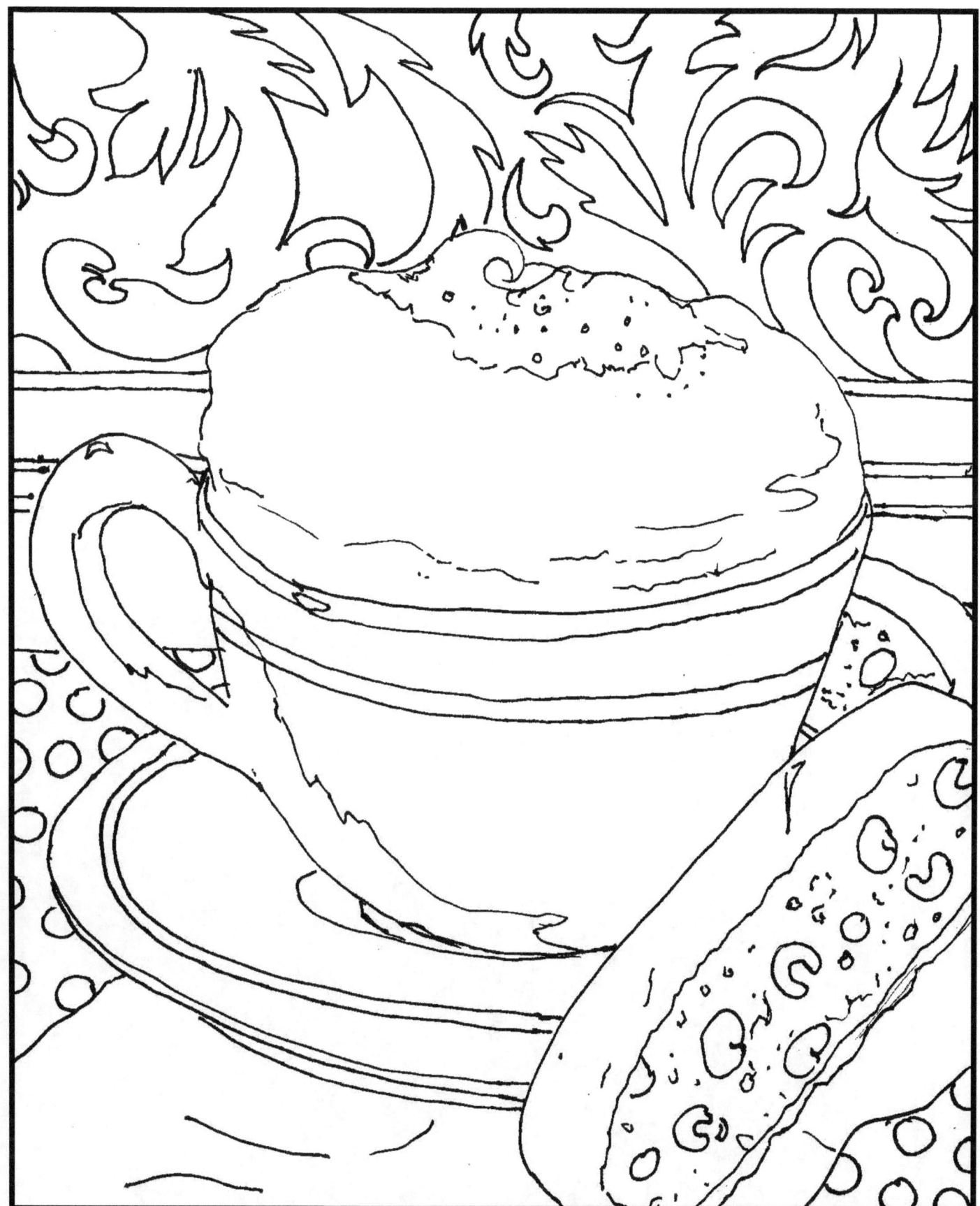

Figure 26 Cappuccino & Biscotti

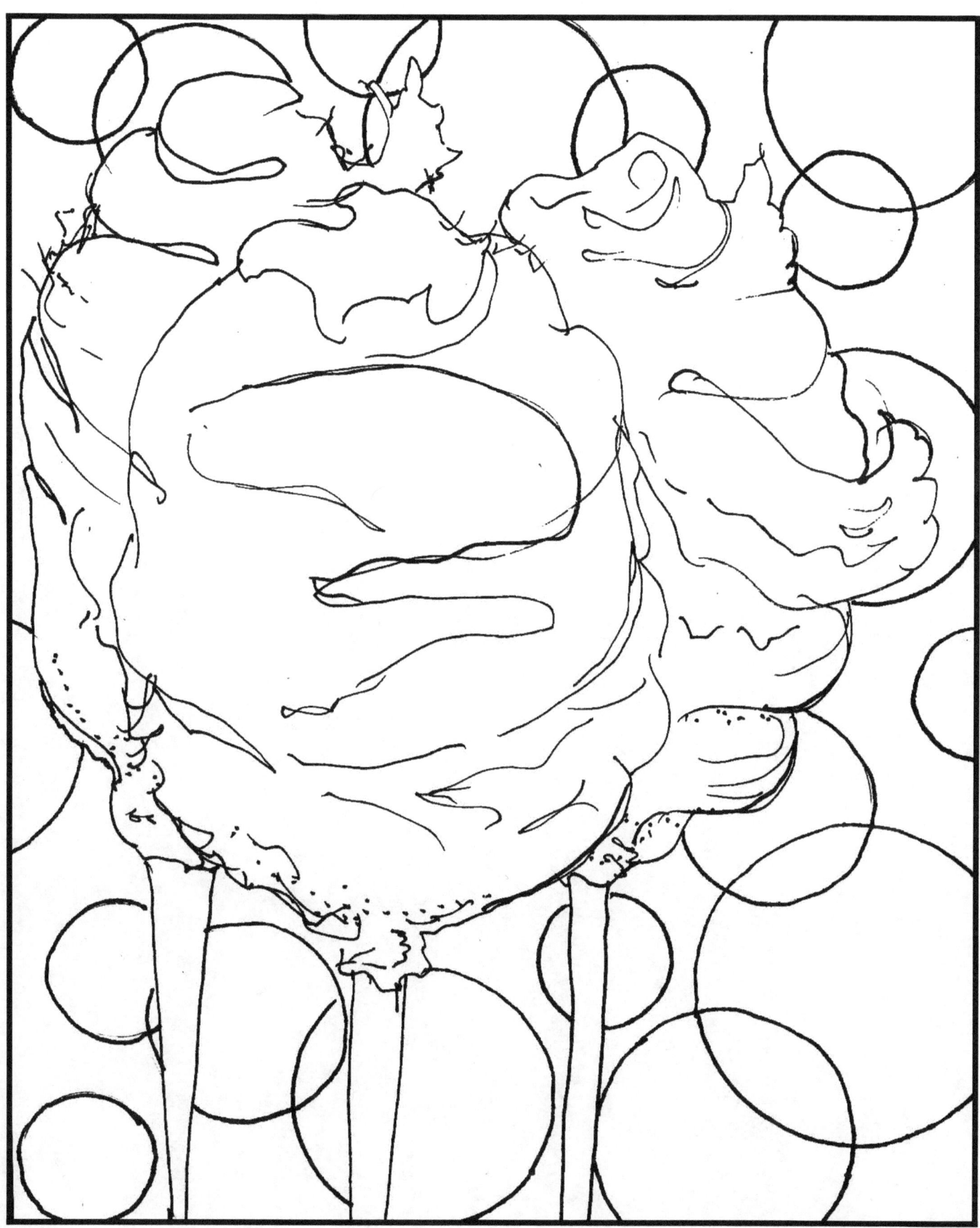

Figure 27 Cotton Candy

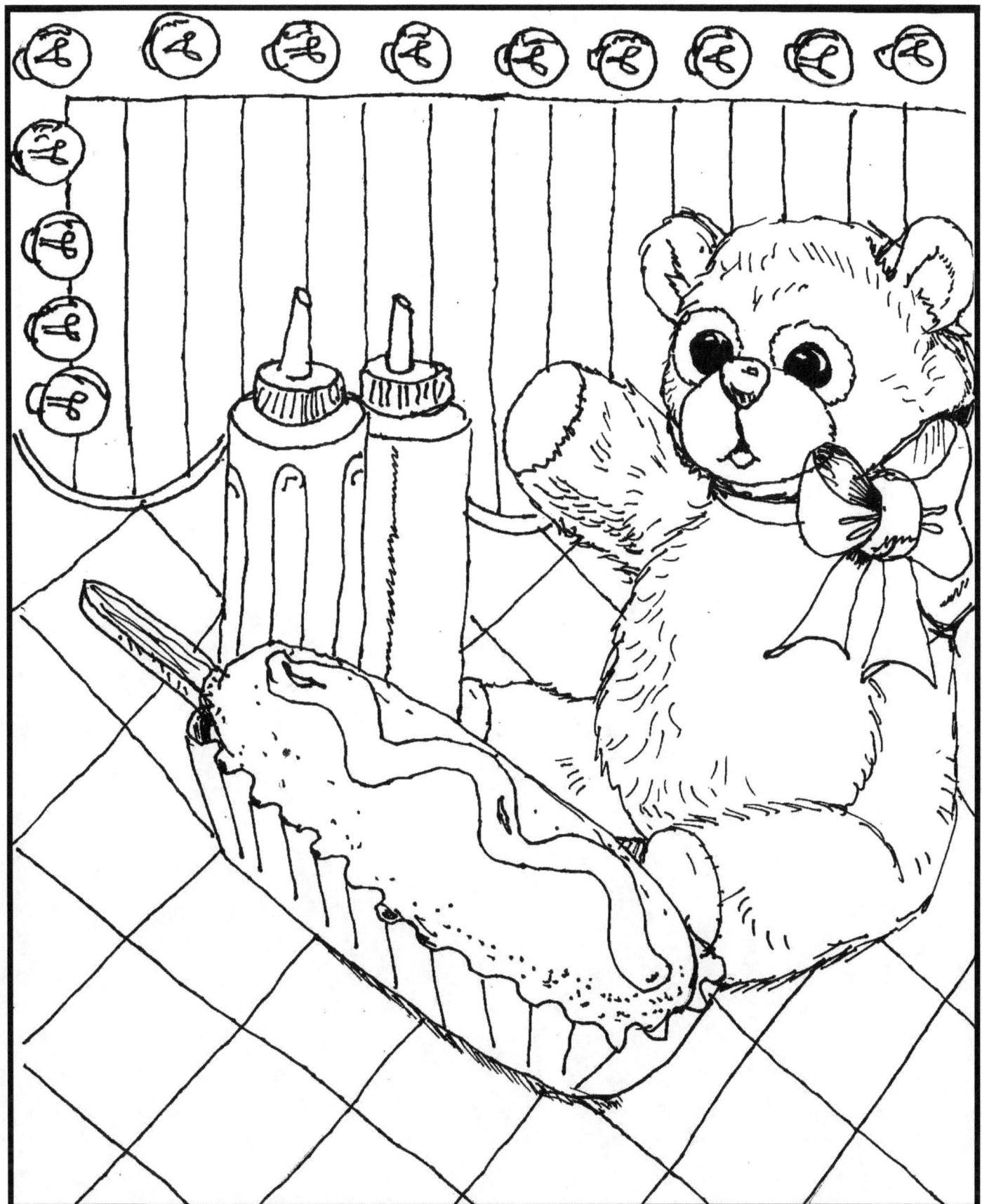

Figure 28 Corn Dog

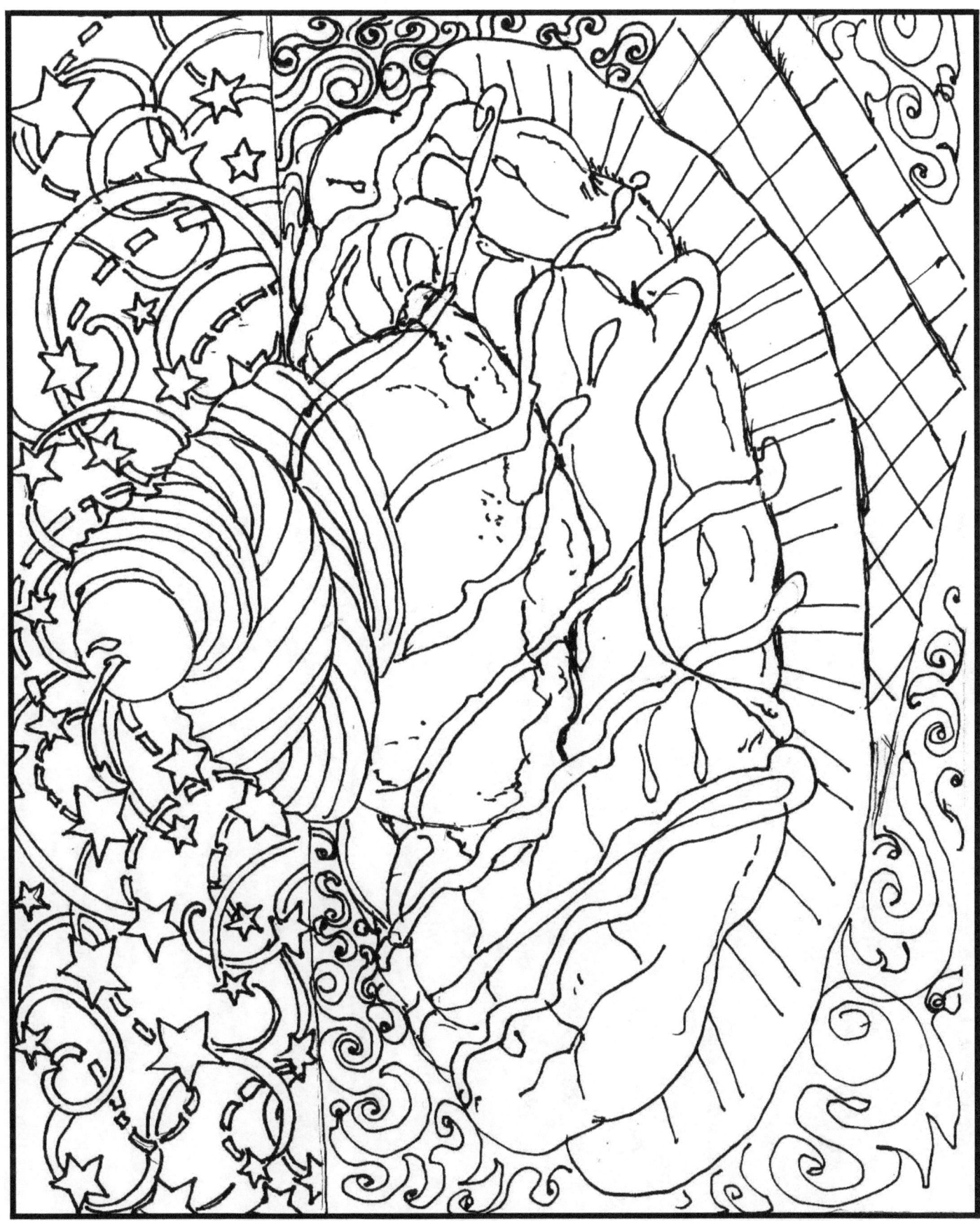

Figure 29 Funnel Cake

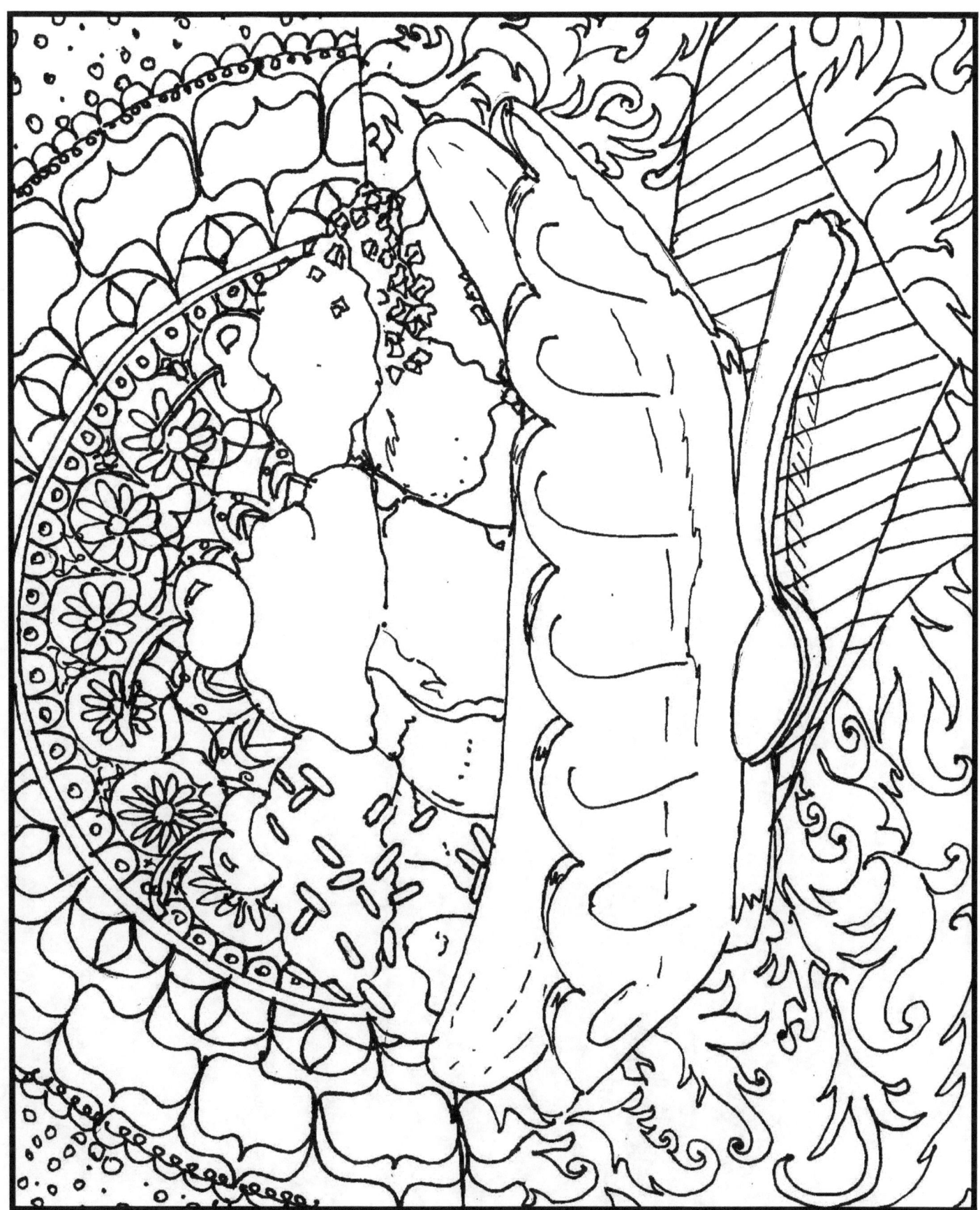

Figure 30 Banana Split

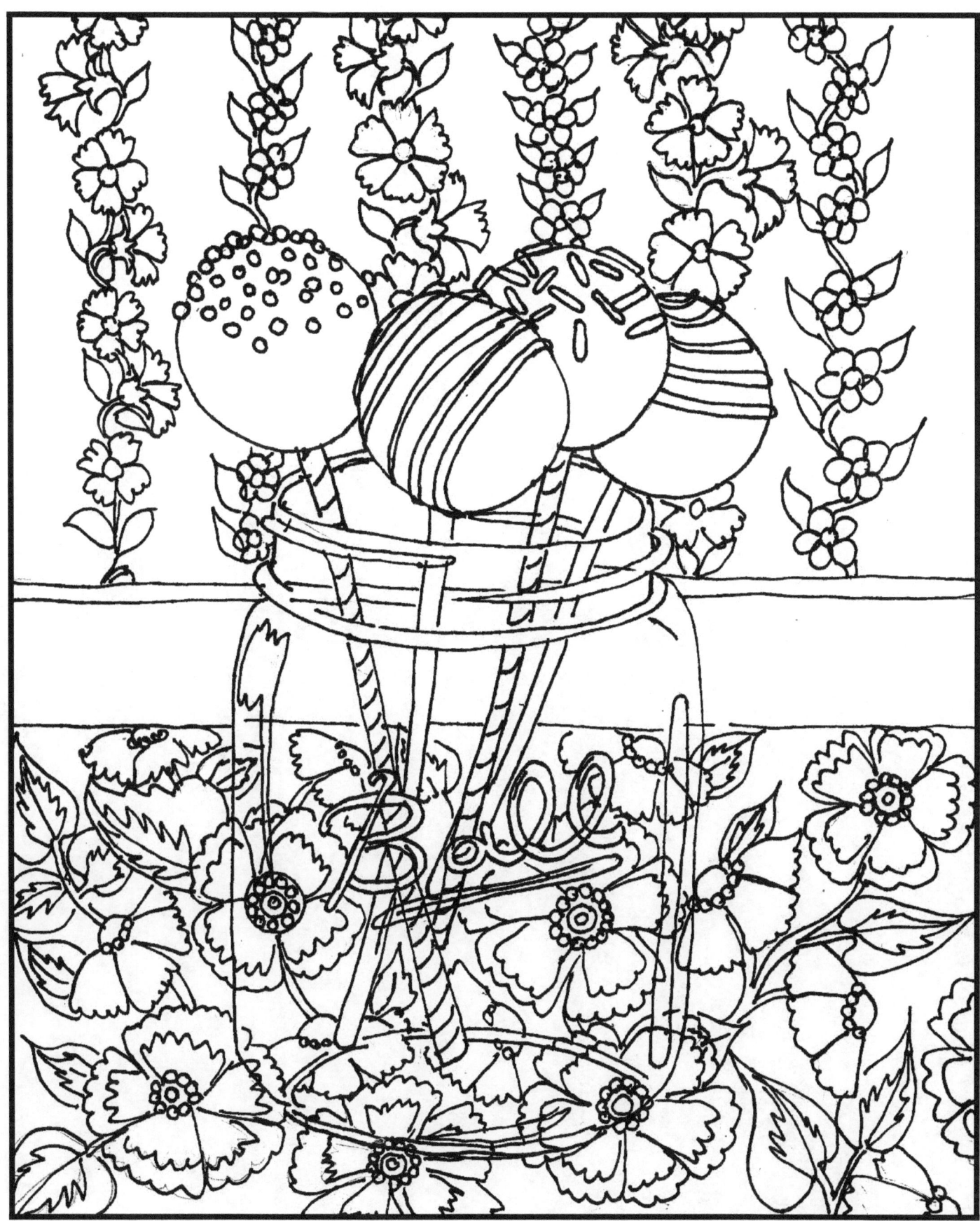

Figure 31 Cake Pops

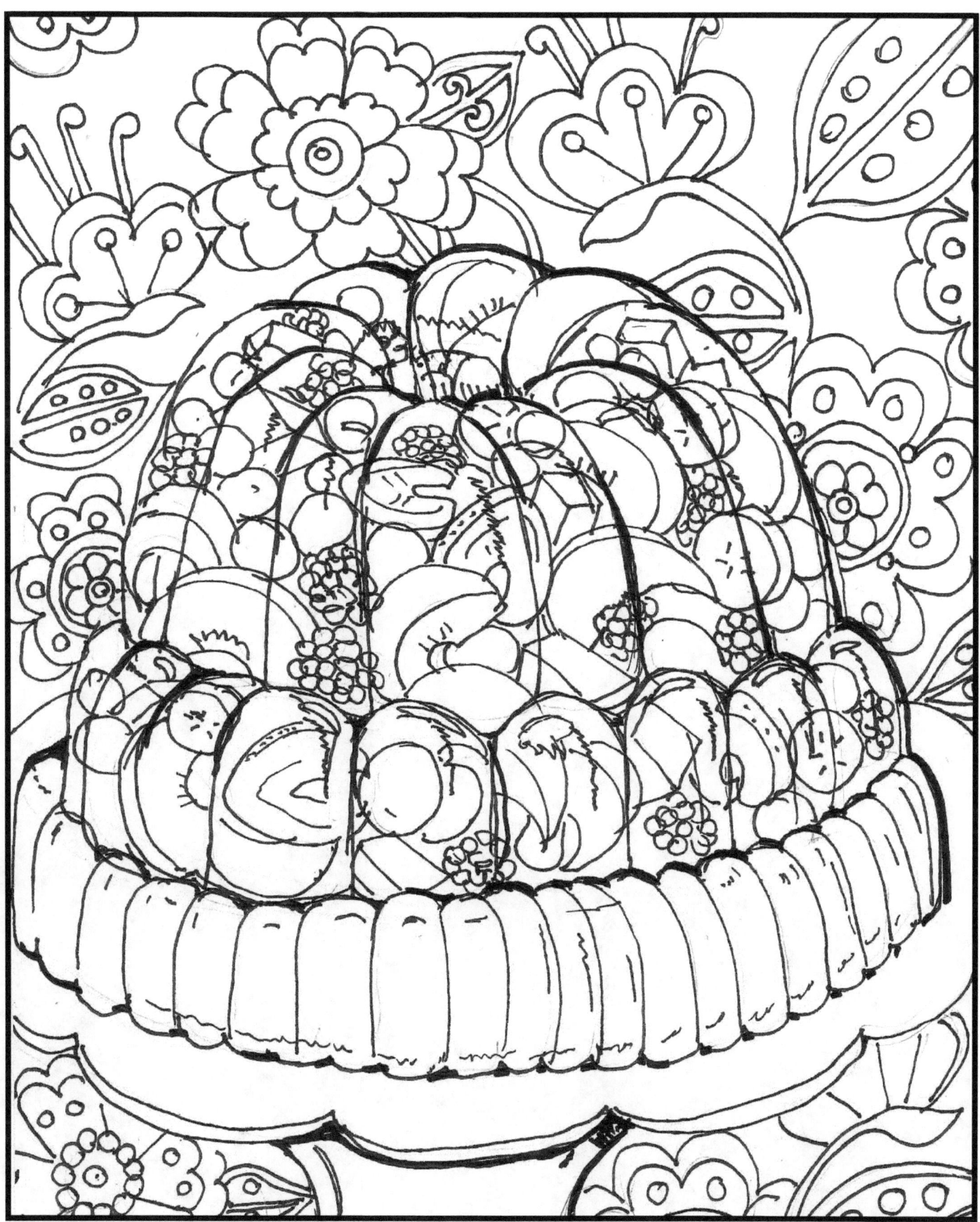

Figure 32 Fruit Jello Mold

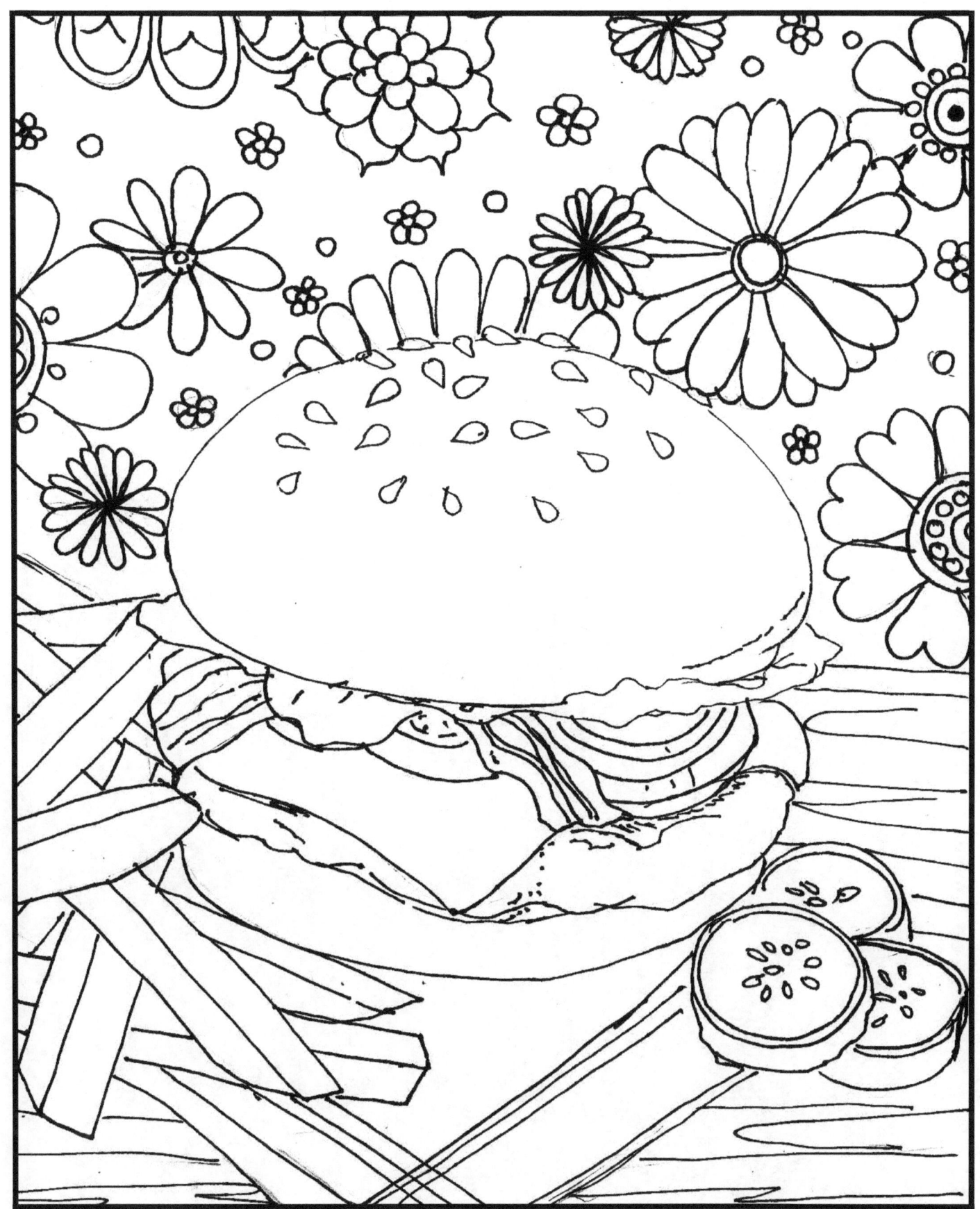

Figure 33 Burger & Fries

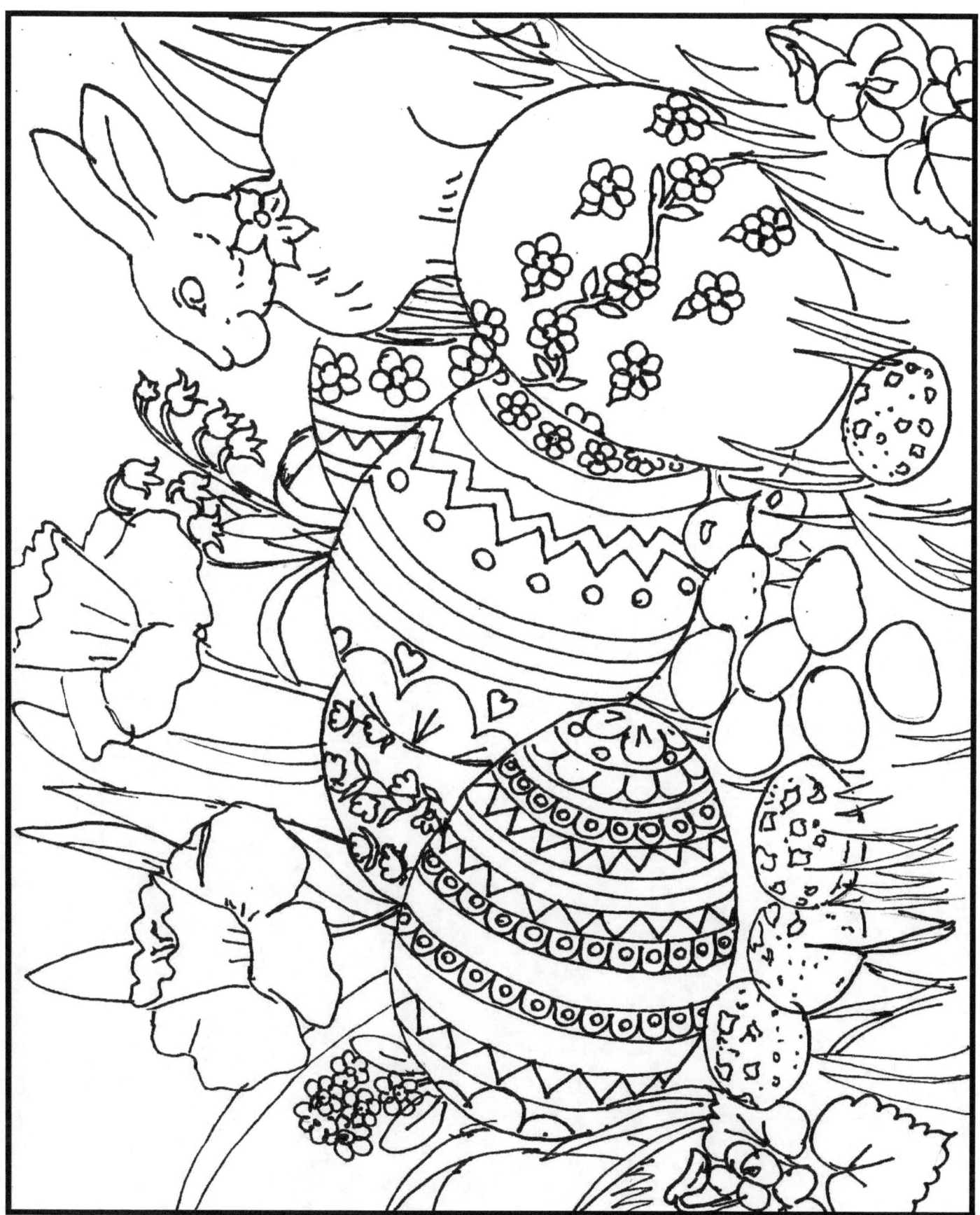

Figure 34 Easter Eggs

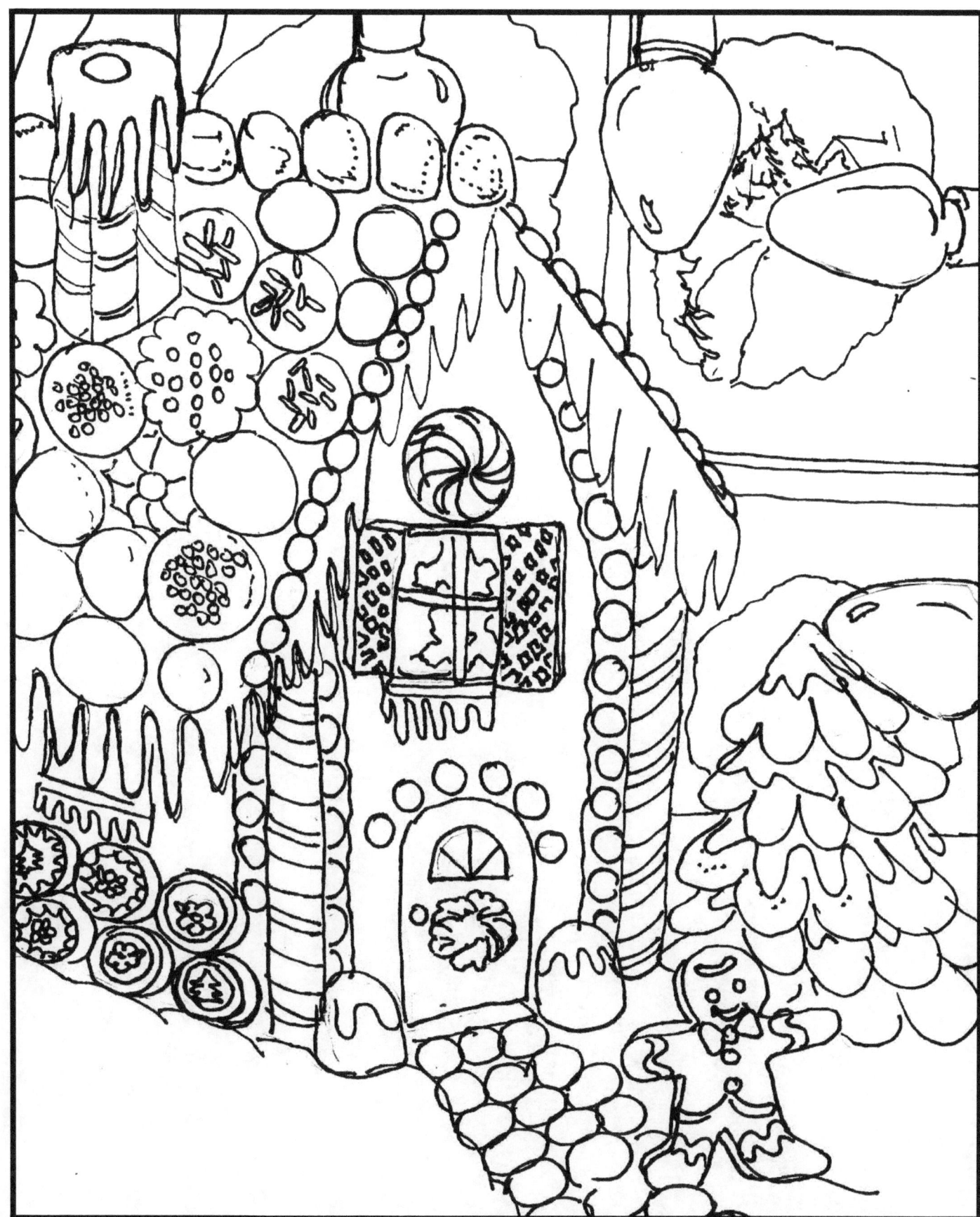

Figure 35 Gingerbread House

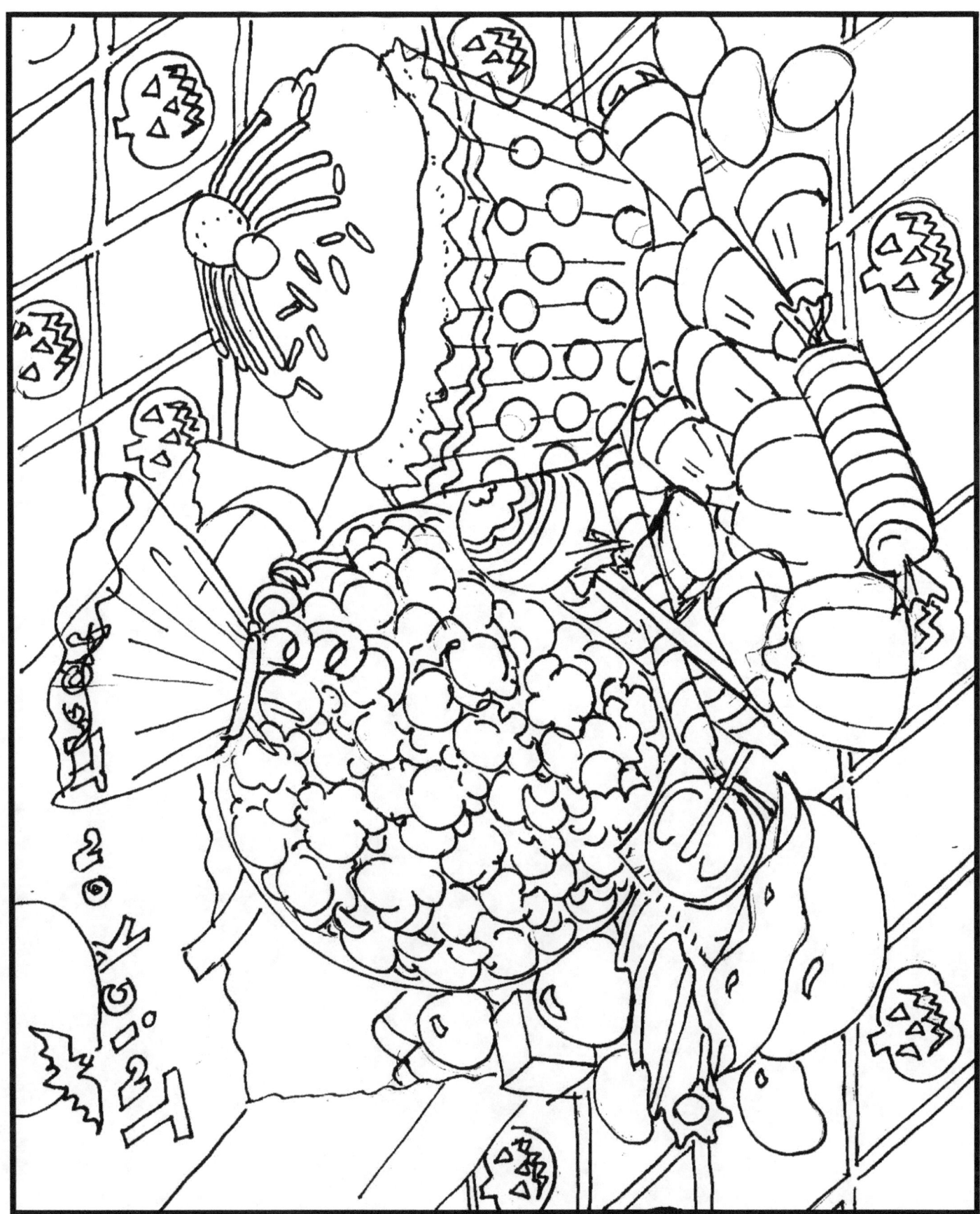

Figure 36 Halloween Candy

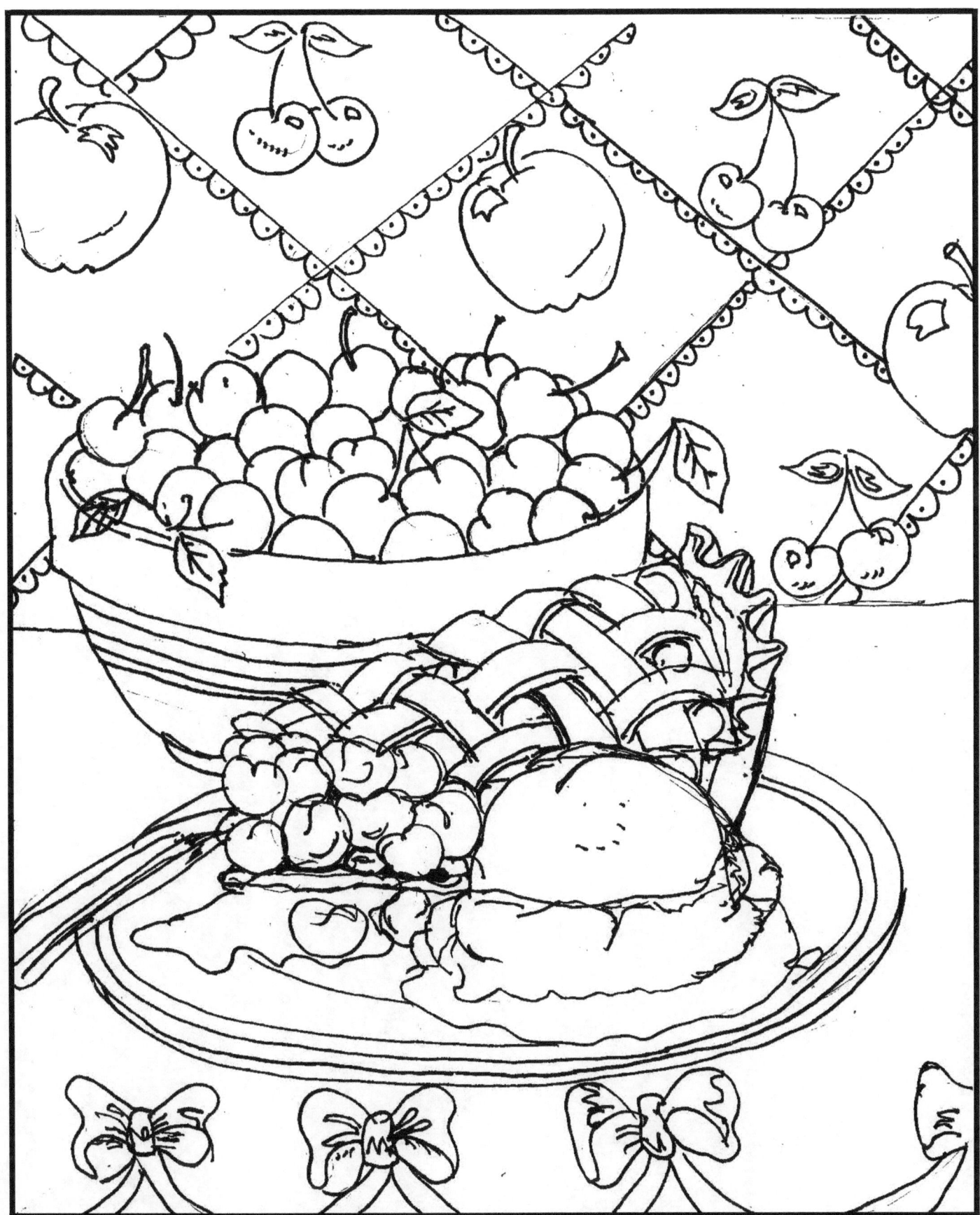

Figure 37 Cherry Pie

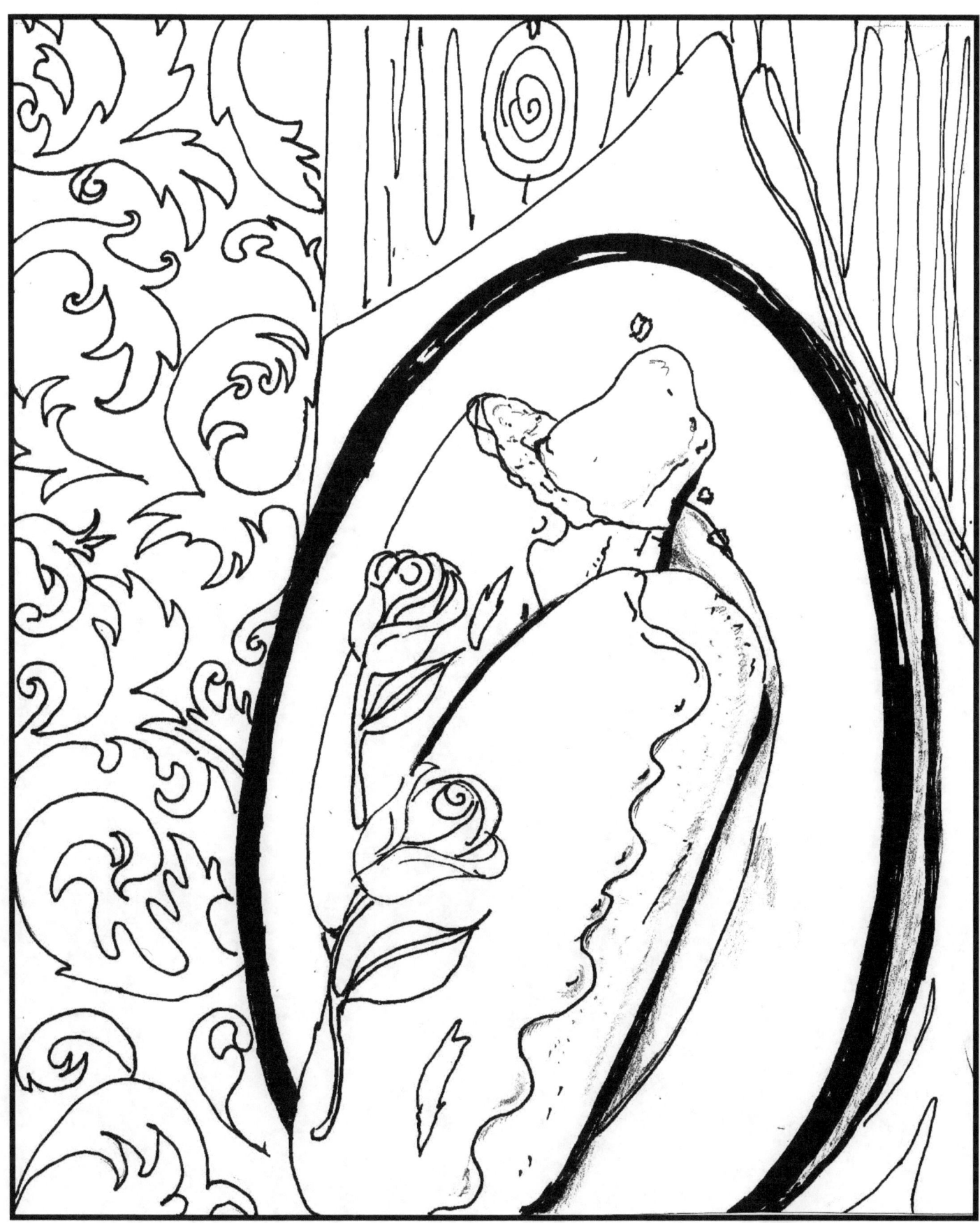

Figure 38 Chocolate Cream Filled Eclairs

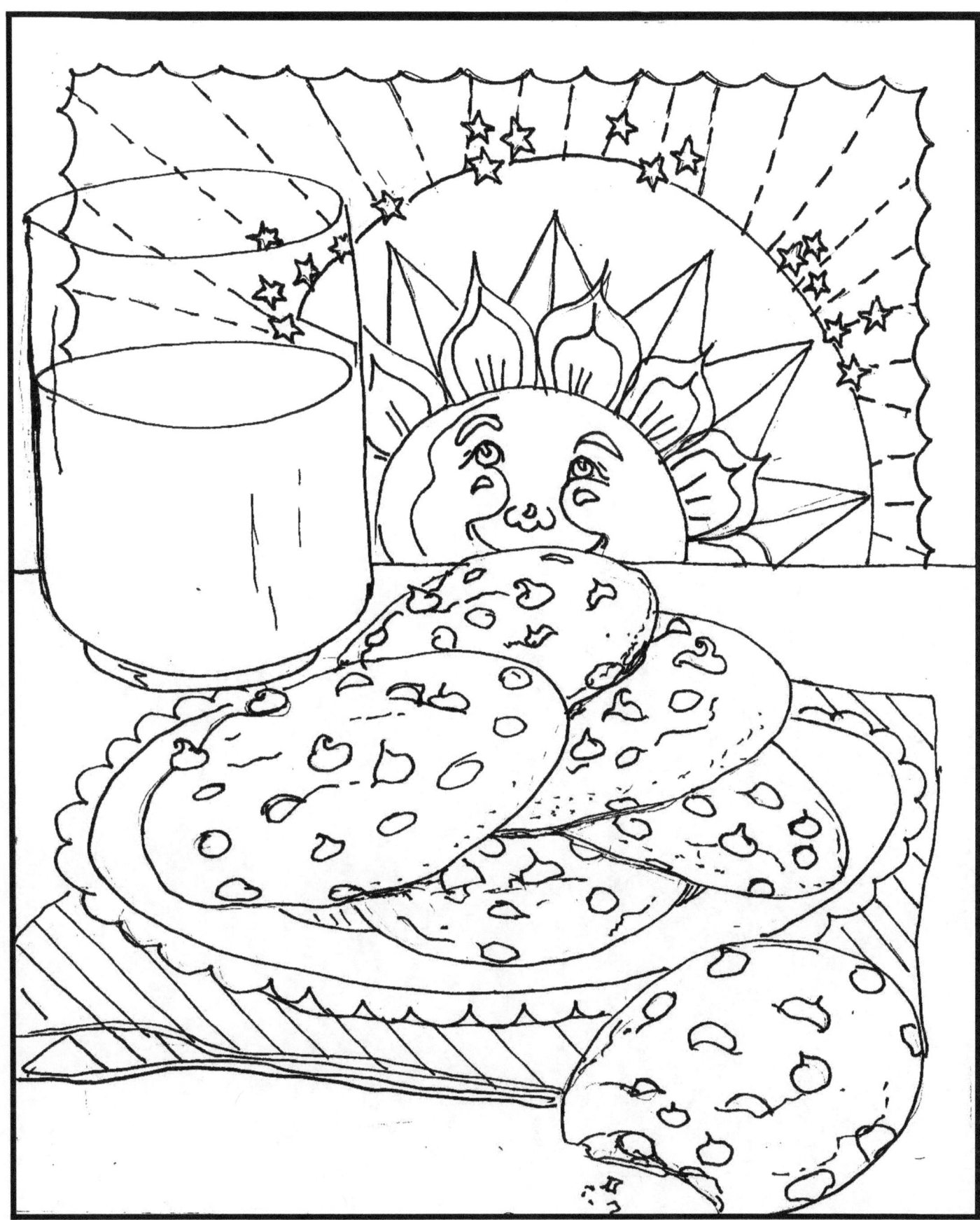

Figure 39 Milk & Cookies

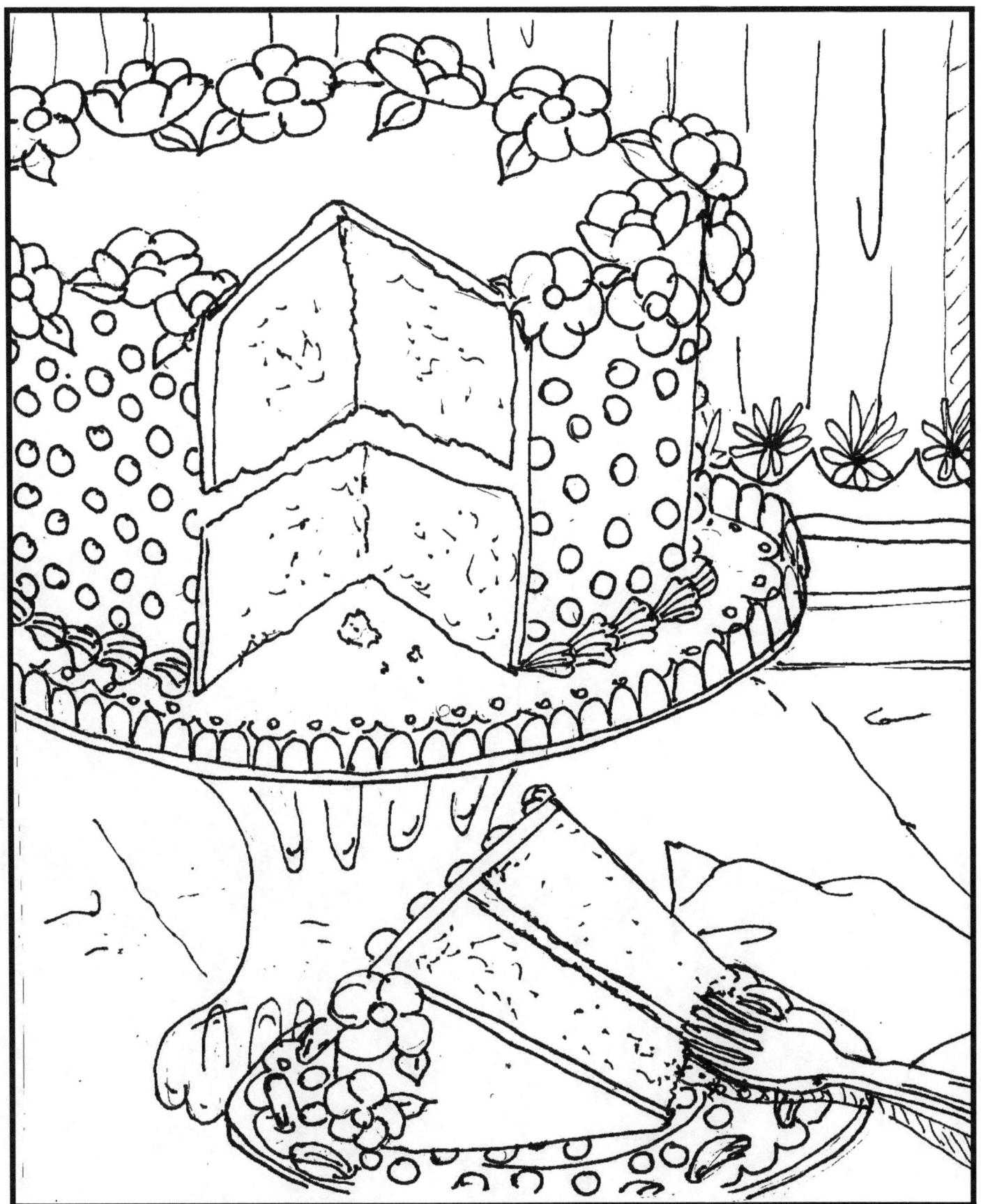

Figure 40 Cake

www.ingramcontent.com/pod-product-compliance
Lightning Source LLC
Chambersburg PA
CBHW080720190526

45169CB00006B/2448

* 9 7 8 1 5 2 3 9 9 2 5 5 3 *